Developing Your Voice

from Personal to Professional

About the author and illustrators

Registered speech-language pathologist **Harald Emgård** started as an actor but early on took an interest in teaching. He has worked in many arenas – from academia to professional – for more than twenty-five years. Formerly Senior Lecturer in Voice and Speech and Principal of Malmö Theatre Academy at Sweden's Lunds Universitet, Harald has worked at a number of theatres and opera houses in Sweden as well as for Swedish Radio and Television guiding actors, dancers, musical artists and opera singers. He is also a regular lecturer at the Speech-language pathologist programs at Lunds Universitet and Åbo Akademi, University of Åbo in Finland. With one foot in the performing arts and the other in the academic field of vocal science, he travels across the world. Working as a vocal coach and lecturer in Taipei, Hanoi, Singapore, Kuala Lumpur, London, Berlin, Florence, St. Petersburg and New York.

Johanna Emgård graduated from The Hebrew University of Jerusalem and is now a PhD student in Medical Science at Karolinska Institutet, Stockholm. She has had many successful exhibitions as a Scientific artist with medical and botanical illustrations as a specialty. Johanna has created the anatomical illustrations.

Wei-Kai Hao graduated from Visual Communication Design department of Yunlin University of Science and Technology. He is an actor, educator and illustrator from Kaohsiung that works regularly in Taipei and Singapore. Wei-Kai has worked with, and translated for, Harald for more than ten years. Wei-Kai has illustrated the exercises.

Developing Your Voice

from Personal to Professional

Harald Emgård

Illustrations by
Wei-Kai Hao and Johanna Emgård

methuen & co

First published in Great Britain in paperback and ebook by
Methuen & Co. 2022

1

Methuen & Co.
Orchard House
Railway Street
Slingsby, York, YO62 4AN
www.methuen.co.uk

Methuen & Co. Limited Reg. No. 5278590

A CIP catalogue record for this title is available from the British Library

ISBN (paperback): 978 0 413 77855 0
ISBN (ebook): 978 0 413 77870 3

Typeset (for paperback and ebook) in Great Britain by
SX Composing DTP, Rayleigh, Essex

Printed and bound in Great Britain by Clays Ltd, Elcograf S.p.A.
Cover design: Brill

Acknowledgements

I would like to thank the following for their support as I worked on this book:

Margareta Unné-Göransson, my senior fellow teacher in Voice and Speech at Malmö Theatre Academy at Lunds Universitet. We worked together for years and talked about teaching and voice. Our joint compendium about voice for the first-year students was the seed for this book.

Sven Bjerstedt from Malmö Theatre Academy and Cia Lundström from the Department of Logopedics, Phoniatrics and Audiology, both at Lunds Universitet. They both read the text and helped me to improve it with questions and remarks and Jonas Andersson offered the same valuable support.

Viveka Lyberg-Åhlander from Åbo Academi University, Finland, Susanna Whitling from the Department of Logopedics, Phoniatrics and Audiology, Birgitta Vallgårda and Barbara Wilczek-Ekholm from the Theatre Academy have had the forbearance to listen and discuss points and subjects in the text.

Deven Ho for the brilliant comparison with cartoons. I 'borrowed' the Beetle from Đỗ Văn Hiền at Vietnam National Opera and Ballet and adjusted it.

Wei-Kai and my niece Johanna's fantastic drawings have made the text more comprehensible.

Hegel Tsai who has interpreted for me during many workshops in Taipei and translated this book into Mandarin.

Alice Vahlén has pruned and tamed my 'Swenglish' into decent English.

Chang Tsai Pao, in Taipei, who challenged me stop talking about writing and do it.

David Sisco, in New York, who has shared his solid knowledge on singing and teaching. David has also been part of some great teaching experiences in New York and Taipei.

Most of all I need to thank Birgitta Vahlén, my colleague and dear friend, who with Argus-eyes read, corrected language, and asked challenging questions. Without her, the result would have been much inferior to the book you now hold.

Last but not least old students, and most of all the students of my early years as a voice teacher. Without them there would be no learning process, no teaching mistakes, no improvements, no experience, and no book to write.

A big thanks to all of you.

Contents

Prologue

When I was a young acting student, I realized that voice and text were where I felt most at 'home.' I never shared the same excitement that my fellow students experienced when on stage and found instead that the only things I truly enjoyed were voice and text classes... and coaching my classmates! It was obvious that I was more drawn to teaching than performing.

After some soul-searching I left the school. What to do now however? Ever since my teens I had dreamed of the theatre yet now my future was uncertain. To support myself I worked as a caretaker at a mental hospital; a fascinating job which gave me important insight into the human mind and emotions, something that helps me in my teaching today.

At the same time, I was a walk-on at the Royal Opera in Stockholm. Later as a speech and language pathology student, I realized I had learned an enormous amount about voice from sharing the stage with the singers night after night; listening to and watching how they worked with their instruments, how they solved vocal challenges and approached different roles. This experience has in many ways shaped my attitude to voice work: I base my work, also with the speaking voice, on the classical singing technique.

I also continued taking singing lessons and lessons in voice, text and acting just for the fun of it. Mimi Pollak (1903–99), one of Sweden's most distinguished acting teachers, taught me how to work with text; how acting cues could be found in rhythm, rhyme and punctuation. She was in her early eighties at the time and generously shared a lifetime of knowledge and experience from a career that had begun in 1922.

Some years later, when it was time to grow up, I attended the speech and language pathology program at Lunds Universitet where I was awarded my degree in medical science. I returned to the world of theatre as a teacher and vocal coach – this time behind the stage instead of on it.

Harald Emgård

Autumn 2022

Introduction

There is nothing mysterious about voice work. We all breathe and use our voices daily and mostly do so without thinking about it. If we want to become skilled voice users we need to start by learning how the voice works – and how we can work in tandem with that function. First of all, we need to find out how we currently use our voice. Thereafter we can develop the voice into a professional instrument. When you work on your voice, do not take short cuts in order to achieve rapid improvement. Take your time to get acquainted with your body and your voice. You need to know what you do with your body and how you do it, thereafter you will be aware of what you already do well and where changes might be required.

The first step in voice training is to achieve a healthy, sustainable and flexible voice. To reach this we need to have the right amount of:

- energy in body and mind
- muscle activity
- air.

Voice work should always be done with a sense of ease and comfort. That does not mean that it can't involve hard work with high physical and mental energy. Hard work, yes, but with a *sense* of ease, a freedom from tensions. You need to work in harmony with your voice, not in conflict with it. When our thoughts, our breath and our voice in speech or singing are effortless we have the ability to reach out to others and touch them with our words and sounds.

When the students I work with, all over the world, suddenly find a healthy and functional way of working with their voice, they look at me in surprise and say, 'but this feels comfortable!' That's right – it should be comfortable!

*

As a voice or singing teacher the most important skill we need to have developed is an analytic listening and a good ability to observe how students use their bodies. We need to be able to hear, see and encourage what students do well, just as much as we need to find what technical shortcomings make the voice less functional. Only then can we – teacher and student together – find the solutions which will guide them to a more healthy and functional voice, and from there develop their voice further.

To find the most suitable exercises for each individual student can be a challenge and it can sometimes take several attempts to find the right fit. Sometimes we can even use the same exercise for different purposes. This makes it imperative that we as teachers are truly familiar with them; know and understand them with our own body before we teach them to someone else. It is not enough with shorter courses or to only read about voice exercises or voice science and thereafter teach from that knowledge. What we teach must be a fusion of scientific knowledge and in-depth skills rooted in ourselves.

This book is an attempt at describing my work and my approach to voice. It is not a description of 'a method.' I am a firm non-believer in trademark methods that promise solve-it-all and guaranteed results. I believe in slow and steady methodical work that is adapted to each individual's needs; a work based on knowledge and under-standing of how the body and voice function. Methods and techniques are the means by which to achieve something, in this case a functional voice. They are not goals in themselves.

*

My teaching focuses on body awareness, posture and breathing and less on the actual sound making. In my experience the order of voice work must be: body → breathing → voice. The body is the most important part of voice work. We easily split between 'me' and 'my body,' but remember that we are a unit of body, thoughts and emotions. Our body reacts to our thoughts and emotions. Stress or happiness affect our body differently, what is going on inside us is expressed through the way we speak and move.

When we speak it always starts with a need or a thought that gives the impulse to express ourselves. That impulse starts an inhalation that is followed by a sound. The impulse will adjust the inhalation to the coming communicative sound. The awareness of what we wish to express prepares the breathing and the sound making system.

This circle is important to keep in mind when it comes to voice training. The impulse for voicing needs to be part of the work, otherwise the exercises easily become mechanical and less efficient.

THE STRUCTURE OF THIS BOOK

This book explains how the voice works – from anatomy, physiology and biomechanics to practical exercises. The anatomical parts are basic; they help you understand the exercises. The international terminology in anatomy is Latin. When there is an established name for the parts in English that name is used with the Latin in brackets. When there is no established word in English I use the Latin directly.

Whenever the sign ➤ appears, it signifies an exercise, something to investigate or try out.

Below that exercise there can be sub-exercises, these are marked by ●.

*

The last chapter consists of some basic thoughts about text and acting. After all, we use the voice to release our thoughts into words. The freedom of the voice that we acquire through exercises is there to support the words, be it our own words or an author's. The range and flexibility of the voice are there to make the words come alive.

HOW TO USE THIS BOOK

This book is written in such a way that you can work on your own with your voice. When training your voice, you start with your voice of today and from there you can develop it further into a skilled instrument; a free, smooth, flexible and sustainable instrument that gives you freedom to express yourself, be it in your personal or professional life.

When I say 'a free voice' I mean a voice that is free from physical, emotional or mental barriers; an effortless and efficient voice.

Skim through the book from beginning to end, so you see how one thing connects with the other. This will give you an overall under-standing of the work. Thereafter, feel free to explore the exercises.

They are basic training and useful for anyone who wants to improve their voice. Investing fifteen to twenty minutes a day doing the exercises will quickly improve your voice. Practicing for a short period of time every day is much better than two hours of hard work once a week.

When you work through the exercises, don't go back and look at the anatomical parts – you need to experience the physical sensations with your body, not your intellect. To learn a craft – a physical knowledge – demands that you actually perform it many times. Reading about it is one part only. It must be experienced:

- Action: do the exercise.
- Experience: pay attention to the sensations.
  What happened in your body and/or mind?
- Reflection: did the exercise matter, did anything change?
- Facts: theoretical explanation.

In some situations, facts can be the start of a learning process. This book is structured with facts first. The aim is to provide a deeper understanding of the exercises that follow. However, do not get stuck on the theoretical part. An approach that is too academic can sometimes stand in the way of the experience of one's own body and voice. It is of course also possible to start with 'Action.' Dive right into the exercise part 'Basic Voice Work' and thereafter go to the beginning of the book and read about how the body actually functions.

The exercises in this book build upon each other, one is the foundation for the other. Take your time and work slowly. Do not move forward until you feel that you have grasped the basics of one exercise. It is then time to venture to the next one, bringing the new skills and awareness with you. Develop your skills step by step:

Do → Experience → Compare → Reflect → Repeat with in-depth understanding and on a new level.

This book doesn't include a vast number of exercises although, since different versions often suit different individuals, there are alternatives to some of them. I find it easier to stick to a handful of exercises and really make them work, to deepen the understanding of them and to explore them fully. In this way, the same exercise can be attempted by a beginner as well as a vocal professional. If you practice the exercises assiduously and wholeheartedly you will find new challenges and new fields to develop in them.

THE LEARNING PROCESS

Developing knowledge or skills goes in a spiral:

- in the first stage, there is no awareness of ignorance;
- in the second stage, there is awareness of the ignorance;
- in the third stage, there is awareness of the new knowledge or skill;
- finally, there is no active awareness of the (new) knowledge, it's become second nature.

You might find the point at which you have awareness of the new knowledge or skill slightly frustrating. The new awareness can even feel disturbing and get in the way of an 'organic' function in the work. Persevere: this frustration will ease when the new skill settles into your body. Remember what it was like learning to ride a bike. When you had mastered balancing and pedalling you turned your attention to the road and the traffic and as such cycling has become a skill you don't think of as mastering, it's become a second nature. Keep in mind that none of us learned to ride a bike just by reading about it or discussing cycling . . . we practiced!

Voice Work

THE VOICE IS A MIX OF ANATOMY AND HABITS

Our voice is a result of our anatomical structures and how we use these structures. The dimensions of the vocal folds (*plica vocalis* in Latin) and resonating systems of each individual are unique. They give us our personal vocal quality – our timbre. These structures are something we can't change. However, the way we use them can be altered. This is our vocal behaviour: how we speak and breathe.

Vocal behaviour is one aspect of how we appear to others. We can control our way of dressing, our gestures and the words we use, but our voice easily gives us away. Think about how we, even on the phone, can immediately hear in a friend's voice that something is out of the ordinary in their life. The voice reflects our inner life more than we realise.

Humans are herd animals and we unconsciously pick up speaking habits (good and bad!) when we adjust to our social environment such as when we're with our family, at school or work or enjoying various leisure activities. The way we speak becomes habitual and we usually have no awareness of it. Our speaking habits become a strong part of our identity. This is an aspect of voice work that in many ways is the most challenging part. A change of vocal habits can be perceived as somewhat of a change in our personality.

*

In too many ways we have a relationship with our body that is influenced by fashion and aesthetic ideals, how we feel we are supposed to look. The same goes for vocal preferences, be it a wish for a deeper voice or a dream of sounding just like our favourite singer. These tastes and ideas seldom benefit the function of the body. We all need to rest with confidence in our own body; we need to experience it and accept it as it is – just as we need to accept our voice as it is.

WORKING WITH THE VOICE

- There is nothing mysterious about voice work. It can be powerful and at the same time straightforward. Simple exercises that you do each day can really improve the voice after only a couple of weeks.

- Our voice expresses what happens inside of us, both physically and mentally. This means that we need to find a way to train the physical processes as well as the thoughts included, so that the voice really does express what we would like it to convey.

- There is no such thing as the 'correct' voice: there is only *my* voice; a healthy voice that gives me freedom to say what I want to.

- The voice is affected by our environment and by our relationship to ourselves and others. It is also affected by what we are hoping to achieve at the given moment.

- We need to find different ways or strategies to use our voice and body, so that we do not inhibit ourselves.

- Voice work takes time since we need to discover both our physical habits and mental habits – our ways of thinking – which create obstacles to the voice reaching its full potential. We also need to find and develop habits and thoughts that benefit our voice, just as we need to recognise and maintain the good habits we already have.

- Voice work is like all physical training: you need to develop consistent routines that help you to maintain your vocal health and skills.

- Taking a proper break from voice work is essential: when at rest new knowledge and skills have time to settle into our mind and body.

- Exercises that free and open the voice can make us feel vulnerable and without our usual 'protection.' This is a very personal work that takes courage.

- Voice work is not about right or wrong but rather it is about exploring and developing the body's abilities.

- Improving the function of your voice can be achieved in a couple of weeks. However, to develop a professional voice – an actor's or singer's voice – is another matter. There are no magical shortcuts; only slow, systematic work.

- The voice changes and develops throughout our life. Life events, habits, age, health, vocal training and professional experience – everything affects the voice. Work with your voice as it is in the moment.

- Change of genre, tessitura or vocal quality, for example from a lyric to a more dramatic voice, needs to be done with respect for where your voice functions best. Try more to follow your voice and develop it slowly, instead of pushing it in a certain direction. This goes for both the daily voice work and the more long-term development of your professional voice.

- We need to equip ourselves with patience and discipline. It takes time to develop skills into something that comes easy and natural for us.

- When you work with your body and voice, accept the state your mind and body are in at the time and work from there.

- Your vocal technique must be so settled in your body and your muscle memory that it takes care of itself. When communicating – on stage or personally – you will have other things to focus on than your vocal technique.

What does it mean to use the voice in a good way?
It means that you can:

- use your voice without damaging it or getting tired;
- use your voice fully and with energy many hours a day and that it is as free and flexible in the end of the day as it was in the beginning;
- express all the nuances and aspects of your thoughts – that you are totally free to express what you wish to say.

Bear in mind that there is no such thing as an ugly voice or a beautiful voice. Let those ideas go, they are taste and social norms. There is only a well-functioning voice or a dysfunctional voice. A free and healthy voice is a *good* voice.

When you are able to link your needs, thoughts, emotions, breath and sound together into one united expression – then you have a good and functional voice. You have *your own* voice.

THE FUNCTION OF THE VOICE

It is important to understand how the body and the voice function – to understand, not to know in detail – when you work with your own instrument. With that understanding, you can achieve greater freedom when trying out new things and decide whether they fit you or not.

The function of the voice, both in speech and singing, is a complex coordination between muscles, mucous membranes and aerodynamics. It is the same physical structures involved regardless of whether the voice is used in speaking or in singing. The differences that exist are more about precision in pitch and duration of the sound. Problems with the 'singing voice' might even be solved by working with the 'speaking voice' and vice versa.

We have the *larynx* in common with many animals. The most basic functions of the larynx and the vocal folds are to protect the lungs from intrusion and to stabilize the torso during hard physical effort. When this is needed the vocal folds close firmly like a valve.

Try this and pay attention to what happens.

> ➢ Lift something very heavy and you will notice that you hold your breath, the vocal folds close fast and hard. Your torso will be more stable and you can lift a bigger weight.

> ➢ Repeat, but this time exhale when you lift, and see how this affects your strength.

VOCAL APPARATUS

The wish to say something initiates an enormous number of impulses in different parts of the brain. A complex and well-coordinated process begins. The impulses are sent into many different parts of the body; from the 'language department' in the brain to the breathing and articulation muscles. Here follows – in a simplified way – how the 'vocal apparatus' works.

Breathing

The inhalation muscles are activated, the torso expands in all directions and the air streams in to the lungs. The exchange of oxygen takes place inside the lungs. When it is time for the air to leave the body the breathing muscles relax, the chest collapses and the volume of the lungs decreases. In this way the air leaves the body. It is a complex cooperation of the many different muscles involved.

In quiet breathing, when we breathe only to oxygenate us, the time phase for inhalation and exhalation is more or less the same.

When we breathe to speak or sing, the exhalation phase is longer than the inhalation phase.

Sound Production

In quite breathing, the vocal folds stay open and the air passes between them as an uninterrupted airflow. In sound production the vocal folds softly close during the exhalation and the outgoing air makes them move. These movements of the folds chop up the air into vibrations. As soon as the air is set in vibration we hear it as a sound.

Sounds can be made without the vocal folds being involved as well. Then it is the articulators that in different ways make the air vibrate. Sounds with the vocal folds involved are said to be *voiced* and sounds where the folds don't vibrate are said to be *voiceless*.

Examine the physical difference.

> Make an [f] sound, then compare it with a [v] sound. Pay attention to the different physical sensations in the throat.

> Make a sustained sound, start on an [f] sound and transform it into a [v] sound, or go from a sustained [s] into a [z] and you will feel how you go from non-vibrating vocal folds to vibration of the folds. You go from *voiceless* to *voiced* sound.

> If you gently feel around the larynx with your fingertips you can feel the vibration starting in the transition from voiceless to voiced sounds.

Resonance and Articulation

The area from the vocal folds in the larynx via the throat to the opening of the mouth and nose is called the *vocal tract*. This area is shaped like a bent tube. We can change the shape of it with our muscles in throat and mouth. The vocal tract is a sound box – an acoustic room – that amplifies the sound waves from the vocal folds. We mould these sounds into meaningful parts, speech sounds, using lips, jaw, tongue, and soft palate – *the articulators*.

VOCAL HABITS: WHERE DO THEY COME FROM?

There is seldom anything wrong with the larynx or the vocal folds when vocal problems arise. Most likely it is more about obstacles in the body and/or the mind. Think of a little child's voice: it is free and uninhibited. There are no blockings or negative habits. When we begin to socialize the expectations from society start to affect us. Blocking habits appear when we go from being content with ourselves to trying to fit in. We adjust ourselves in the effort to satisfy demands, real or imagined, from people around us. We then easily inhibit ourselves as we strive to fulfil those expectations. Our mind affects the body which in turn affects the voice: we breathe less freely and our voice can't work to its full potential.

Ineffective vocal behaviour can also come from temporary vocal problems such as a cold that makes us hoarse, or other difficulties that lead to compensatory vocal behaviour. These behaviours can settle into our vocal habits.

To work with the voice means to be aware of, and to let go of, all blocking habits, habits that can be deeply embedded in us. This can make the work feel uncomfortable, even threatening.

One of the reasons that a feeling of discomfort might appear in voice work is that our life history, our experiences and our personality are reflected in the voice. The need to feel secure or comfortable makes us easily cling to our habits. They have become automatic and we are unaware of them. Because of this lack of awareness, it might be hard to discover our vocal habits and to let go of the less functional ones. Sometimes they can even give us secondary benefits – for example, people might be kinder to someone with a small and fragile voice.

When we change our voice or our way of speaking, friends and family can react negatively. They might feel that we have changed personality. It is not uncommon with remarks such as 'you sound strange nowadays.' Do not let this bother you; they will eventually get used to your new way of speaking.

*

If we do not dare, or allow ourselves, to take our place – our space – among other people, we might hold back our voice and our breathing. Different cultures have their own social rules and conventions for what is seen as appropriate or not. It can be anything from our country's laws and traditions, to the values of family and friends. Speaking with a free and clear voice against the current norms or the established and accepted 'truth' is not an easy thing to do.

> All of us have occasionally stopped ourselves from speaking freely. Try to remember when that has happened to you and see if you can recall the situation – and what happened to your breathing and voice.

> Think about how you breathe in different situations in life. How does this affect your body and mind and your way of speaking?

If we can stop blocking ourselves our body and voice will work as a unit. As long as we emotionally protect ourselves the breathing will not be free. If the breathing is not free, the voice will depend upon compensatory muscle work in throat, neck, tongue and jaw. This leads to limitations in the resonance and in the flexibility of the voice.

Breathing deep and freely helps us connect to our body and our inner life – our thoughts and emotions. It increases our presence and charisma. This matters not only to actors, it is important for anyone who wants to be heard. Furthermore, a free body facilitates a free mind, something that benefits our creativity and fantasy. It is crucial to remind ourselves that all of us have the right to speak, the right to take our place and space, and we all have the right to take the time needed to do so. There is no vocal technique in the world that will make you be heard unless you want to be listened to – and allow yourself the right to speak out.

Voice Science

This chapter covers anatomy and physiology of the body. There is also a basic explanation of acoustics and a section about the confusing terminology around register.

It is important to have a general understanding of the parts of the anatomy that affect the breathing system and the voice production. It facilitates the voice work and the ability to understand and implement exercises in an optimal way.

THE LOCOMOTOR SYSTEM

The locomotor system consists of two parts: the skeleton and the muscles.

The Skeleton

The skeleton's function is to support the soft parts of the body, to protect the inner parts and to function as a lever for the skeletal (striated) muscles. The joints connect different bones in the skeleton and they can bend, rotate or slide – or make a combination of these movements.

The spine consists of thirty-four vertebraes and can bend forwards, backwards and sideways. It can also stretch a little and rotate on its own axis.

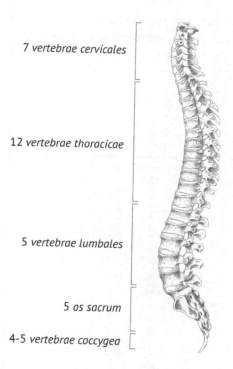

7 *vertebrae cervicales*

12 *vertebrae thoracicae*

5 *vertebrae lumbales*

5 *os sacrum*

4-5 *vertebrae coccygea*

The spine supports the head, shoulders, arms and thoracic and abdominal organs. The convex shape of the spine relieves the burden of the back. The spine is the core of the torso. The weight of the torso is transferred through the hip joint to the femur, from the femur through the knee to the lower leg and from the lower leg through the ankle joint to the foot.

However, in voice work you must think the other way around. Instead of having the weight pushing down on us, we balance on the feet and retrieve the stability from the ground. Through the feet and ankle joints we stack and balance the lower legs; on top of the lower legs we have the knees, through them we stack and balance the femur; on top of them, through the joint of the hips, we stack and balance the pelvis. From the pelvis we stack all thirty-four vertebraes one by one and so balance the spine; from the spine hang the ribcage, the shoulders and the arms; finally on top of the spine we balance the head.

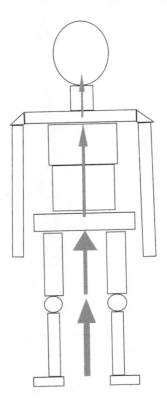

Muscles

We have three versions of muscles. Two of them belong to the locomotor system: the smooth and the skeletal muscles. The third version is the cardiac muscles. We are unable to control the smooth and the cardiac muscles at will; they belong to the involuntary system of the body. Smooth muscles can contract spontaneously after being passively stretched. This recoiling is part of our breathing.

The skeletal muscle group is the one we usually think of when we talk about muscles. They can contract, relax or slowly give in from contraction. They can also be passively drawn out – stretched. They attach via tendons on either side of the joints and in this way function as levers.

Muscles that connect to the same skeletal parts and affect a certain joint are often organized into muscle groups. Muscles that have the same function and assist each other in their work are called synergists.

If you bend your arm the biceps in your upper arm contracts and at the same time the triceps relaxes. To stretch the arm the opposite takes place; biceps relaxes and triceps contracts. Here the biceps and the triceps work as antagonists to stabilize the movement. The active contracting muscle is called agonist and the relaxing or lengthening muscle is called antagonist. This antagonistic cooperation occurs in most movements in the body.

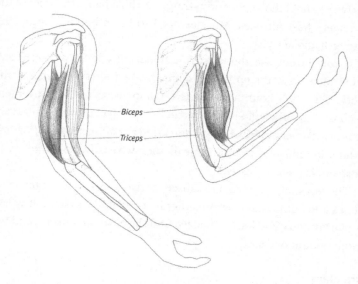

Biceps

Triceps

> Lift a dumbbell; bend and stretch the arm in a slow, smooth and controlled motion. You will notice how the muscles cooperate. One of them contracts and the other slowly gives in.

The function of the skeletal muscles is to work actively and thereafter relax. It is when they are in constant low activity that we have tensions in them and they become sore. If we were to only use them for active work and then relaxed them there would seldom be any soreness. Think of the shoulders that often are a little raised all the time, in constant activity. Most of us have tensions and some pain there.

Muscles also work in a chain reaction: what one muscle is doing affects the muscle connected to the other side of a joint or bone. The pain in a sore muscle may actually have its origin in another muscle. For example, chest muscles that are stronger than back muscles might lead to pain around the shoulder blade and neck. This is because the weaker back muscles are forced to be in permanent activity to hold the upper body straight; to hold back the effect of the stronger chest muscles. Muscles need to be in balance regarding strength and activity.

If you do not use the most functional muscle for a movement, other muscles will step in and compensate and try to support the work. This is a counterproductive compensation; the movement becomes less efficient and can result in tension in the compensatory muscles. For example, when we don't find the efficient and effortless exhalation muscles when we speak, then we easily tense and try to push out the sound instead.

The locomotor system is a closely networked system of muscles, bones and joints that work together in a chain like system. It works smoothly and effortlessly when we find the optimal muscles and the right amount of energy.

Breathing

There are two cavities in the torso; the thoracic cavity, located inside the rib cage, and the abdominal-pelvic cavity. They are closely related during breathing and function in a way as antagonistic units to each other. They are both separated and united by the diaphragm.

Movement in one of these cavities affects the shape and function of the other one. In the thoracic cavity we have among other things heart (*cor,* or *kardia* in Greek) and lungs, and in the abdominal cavity we have the stomach and intestines.

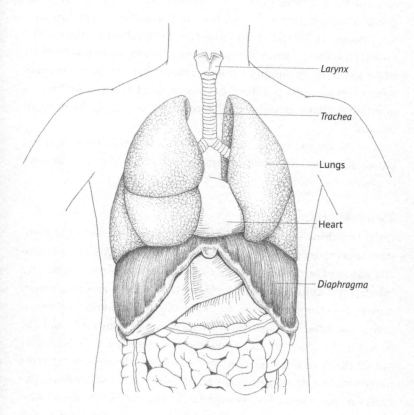

Lungs

The primary function of the lungs (*pulmo*) is to oxygenate us for survival; that is where the exchange of oxygen (in) and carbon dioxide (out) takes place. For the air to enter and exit the lungs a complex cooperation of muscle activity takes place. The lungs are sponge-like and divided into two pleural sacks. The sacks consist of two layers and the outer layer sticks to the diaphragm, the ribs and the breastbone. Lung capacity varies considerably between individuals. Total capacity is somewhere between four to seven litres of air; a relaxed breathing provides around half a litre of air going in and out. On average we breathe fifteen breaths per minute. It is impossible for us to fully empty the lungs, there will always be air left (*residual volume*). When you feel as if you have run out of air when speaking or singing – you haven't. What you have probably done is tense up so you don't have access to the air available. It's more likely that you have much more air left than only the residual volume.

It is impossible to increase the size of the lungs, since they are mostly surrounded by bones. However, we can increase the efficiency of how we use the air.

Quiet breathing

Quiet breathing is controlled by the *medulla oblongata* in the brain stem and is part of the autonomic nervous system. We are not usually aware of our breathing and cannot totally control it. When we inhale, the diaphragm (*diaphragma*) activates. When the diaphragm muscle contracts, it lowers. To give space for this lowering movement, the different muscles of the abdominal wall relax and the abdominal viscera (stomach and intestines) move a little bit down-out. At the same time the outer layer of the muscles between the ribs (*intercostales externi*) activates and the ribs are elevated out-up. The cavity of the chest (*thorax*) expands in three different directions: downwards, forwards and to the sides. As a result, the lungs, which are elastic and stick to the inside of the ribcage and the diaphragm, also expand. The air pressure inside them decreases and becomes lower than the atmospheric pressure that surrounds us. This leads to air from the outside streaming in, to balance the difference between the outside and the inside air pressure. We inhale.

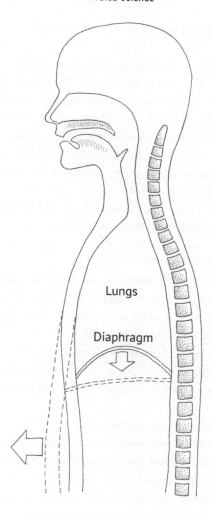

Lungs

Diaphragm

Then comes the exhalation. The diaphragm relaxes and elevates to its original position. The viscera return in-up in the abdomen. The outer muscles of the ribs relax and the ribs sink down-in and constrict the cavity of the chest. The elasticity of the lungs recoil. The lungs decrease and the air pressure increases. When the pressure becomes higher than the atmospheric pressure the air streams out. We exhale.

In quiet breathing, the cavity decreases mainly because the muscles of respiration relax. In this way the volume of the lungs decreases and the air streams out. After a passive exhalation there comes a moment of relaxation before the next inhalation begins. All through these phases the vocal folds stay open. The interplay between the different air pressures is called Boyle's Law.

When speaking or singing the breathing is brought up to a conscious level. The activity can then be modified and developed through training. The exhalation during quiet breathing is largely passive but in speech and singing it is active.

Breathing in voice production

The respiratory system involves not only the diaphragm and rib muscles, but also groups of muscles in the abdomen and the back. There are also crucial muscles deep down in the pelvis that assist the breathing. In addition, exhalation is helped by the smooth muscles and the tissue of the lungs; they stretch while inhaling and recoil during exhaling. The abdomen and the diaphragm work as an antagonistic unit and so do the inner and outer layer of the inter-costal muscles.

The diaphragm is the biggest and the primary muscle in breathing. It is a big, arched muscle plate that sticks to the inside of the ribs, the lower part of the breastbone and to the vertebrae in the height of the belly button. The diaphragm divides the torso into one over and one under part. It is important to remember that the diaphragm is an inhalation muscle. If we tense it during exhalation we actually start an inhalation at the same time as the exhalation is ongoing. In this way we block the free outgoing flow of air and tense up instead of staying open and free. This is usually what happens when we feel like we have run out of air. Metaphorically, we simultaneously press the accelerator and the brake.

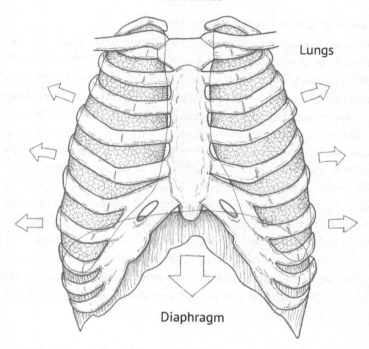

Lungs

Diaphragm

To keep control over the sound when speaking or singing, all these muscles must constantly adapt their activity in relation to how much air there is left in the lungs. If the muscle activity were static every phrase would start off loudly and then quickly go down in volume, ending in something like a creak.

In sound production the outgoing stream of air is held back slightly by the muscles used for inhalation, mostly by the rib muscles and the muscles in the back. This holding-back work is how we keep control over the air pressure under the vocal folds (subglottal air pressure, more about that later). This is the base in what is generally known as the *support* of the voice.

The cooperation between the diaphragm and the abdominal wall creates movements in the intestines. This stimulates the peristalsis and may cause some interesting sounds from the stomach.

A sound production phase, step by step

When we prepare for a long phrase we take a deep breath. The air-pressure in the lungs is high, and if not held back the air would stream out fast and create a loud voice which would fade away quickly. The muscles used for inhalation keep their activity and keep the torso expanded, and in this way hold back the outgoing air flow so that we have control over the air. Step by step the amount of air drops and the air pressure in the lungs decreases. We hold back less and less, until the moment of equilibrium in the air pressure.

Thereafter, we need to activate the muscles of exhalation instead. We need to both increase the activity and involve more muscles. In this way we make sure that the air continues to stream out even when, in a relaxed breathing, it would be time for an inhalation. We let out the air actively instead of passively. This activity makes the airflow below the vocal folds stay steady and yet flexible during the phrase, something that is important for control of pitch and volume.

*

All of this works as a well-integrated unit. When the body is uninhibited and prepared to create a sound, the muscles cooperate with each other. It is contra productive to put time and effort into trying to take hold of each muscle group involved.

*

Here comes, for the inquisitive, an illustration of the activity pattern of the main breathing muscles. This is not an exact scientific description. The patterns of breathing and voice making are also a bit individual.

The diagram shows first two quiet breaths and then a big inhalation to prepare for the long phrase that follows.[1] Then comes a big intake as a recovery after the long exhalation and finally a further quiet breath.

---

1 The illustration is based on Lindblad (1992) and Ladefoged (1967).

In the long exhalation you can see how more and more muscles activate while the air leaves the body. Thereafter comes the big intake as a recovery after the long exhalation, since the body always strives to go back to equilibrium.

In the standing axis in the diagram there is a mark (+/-) where equilibrium in the air pressure occurs. This is the moment in sound production where the inhalation muscles relax after the holding back function and the exhalation muscles are activated.

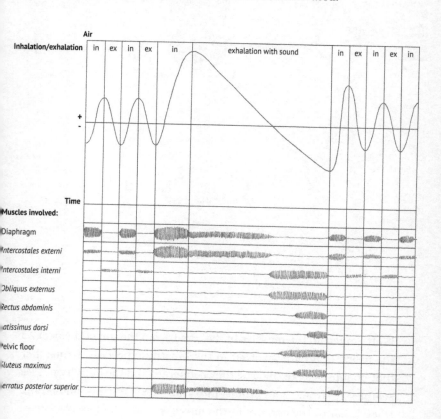

The muscles work in a closely knitted net and affect each other. Many of them attach to a common bone such as the spine, ribs or pelvis. They all function as a unit.

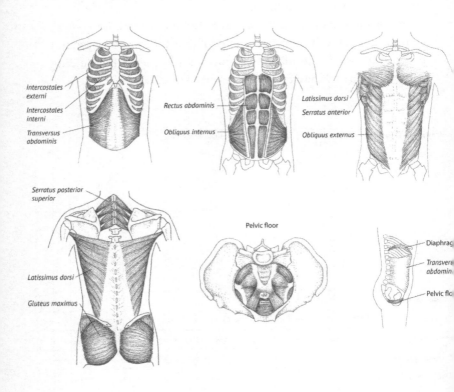

Pretty much all the muscles in the torso, from the top of the neck to the pelvic floor, are involved in the breathing process. Remember that no muscles are soloists: they cooperate and the activity passes seamlessly from one group into the next during phonation. In addition to the activity in the muscles come the passive forces: elasticity in smooth muscles and tissues together with the gravity. These too assist during exhalation.

Which muscles are activated, and to what degree, depends on what we do with the voice. Relaxed speaking or heightened speaking from a stage, a high note in opera or a lullaby, they all require different activity. Furthermore, we all have our individual differences in how we use our instrument, our body.

A way of thinking about all of these respiratory muscles is to imagine a rectangular 'breathing-box' inside your chest with six sides: front-rear (chest-back), top-bottom (neck-pelvic floor) and right-left side. Each of these should be moveable in breathing. The different sides will not be activated all the time or have the same amount of activity, but you need to be in contact with them during the inhalation and keep that contact/awareness throughout the phrase. This is done by finding the right way to inhale – with a deep releasing of the muscles. In this way, they are all 'on duty' from the start and ready to step in, when the voice needs extra support.

You need to experience all this with your body, not with your intellect. Trust your body. Allow it to work in its natural way.

THE LARYNX

The larynx is located in the neck, level with the third to sixth cervical vertebrae. It is situated below the throat (*pharynx*) and on top of the windpipe (*trachea*) and consists of a framework of cartilages bound together by ligaments, mucosal membrane and muscles. It is suspended from the bone of the tongue – the hyoid bone (*os hyoideum*). The larynx is flexible and can move up and down a little, like when we swallow or yawn. Inside the larynx are the vocal folds. They are two lip-like folds located horizontally in the direction face-neck. The primal function of the larynx and the vocal folds is to protect the lungs from anything other than air entering them.

I tend to avoid talking about the larynx and its function, focusing more on breath and resonance. My experience is that too much discussions of the larynx can tie up the singer or speaker. By contrast, some vocal techniques give explicit instructions about the larynx to achieve particular sounds. These more prescriptive approaches, while sometimes creating immediate results, have the potential to keep the singer from discovering a more natural way of voicing through their body awareness.

Outside larynx

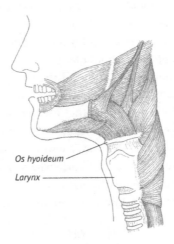

Os hyoideum

Larynx

The extrinsic laryngeal muscles are involved in some singing techniques, via indirect impact on the inner muscles of the larynx. The muscles below the larynx can stabilize it when high air pressure is used, such as in belting or dramatic singing on high notes and with high intensity.

The outer laryngeal muscles can move the larynx a maximum of two centimetres up and down. The muscles above the larynx (extrinsic suprahyoid muscles) are connected to the base of the skull and the tongue bone. They raise the larynx. The muscles below the larynx (extrinsic infrahyoid muscles) are connected to the top of the breastbone (*sternum*) and collarbone (*clavicula*). They lower the larynx.

Outside of, and around, these extrinsic laryngeal muscles we have a network of muscles in the neck. They are connected to the skull, collarbone, breastbone and shoulders and control the movements of the head. All of these muscles can affect the position and function of the larynx. Therefore, don't forget to relax neck and shoulders during the exercises.

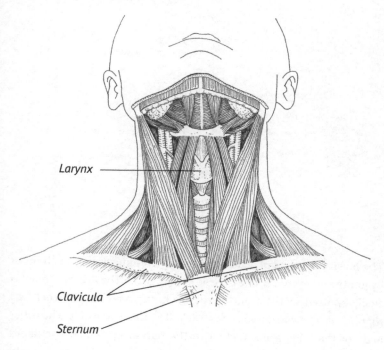

Larynx

Clavicula

Sternum

Epiglottis

Directly above the larynx, and at the rear of the hyoid bone, is the epiglottis. It is a leaf-like cartilage anchored in the root of the tongue and in one of the cartilages inside the larynx. Epiglottis folds down over the larynx when swallowing and thus directs the food or fluid into the gullet (*oesophagus*). There are some theories which suggest that this structure is actively involved in phonation and resonance. How epiglottis is involved as a resonator is not quite known but at least in laboratorial experiments it seems like epiglottis might affect sound intensity.

Inside larynx

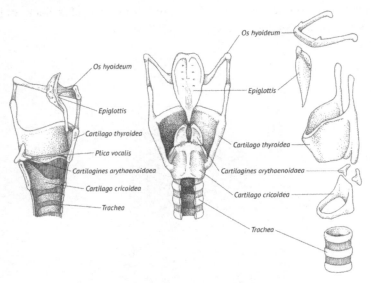

The larynx consists of different cartilages connected to each other by joints and muscles. The thyroid cartilage (i.e. the Adam's apple) is easily spotted at the front of the neck on some people (*cartilago thyroidea*). The vocal folds are attached to the inside of it. The other ends of the folds are attached to the paired arytenoid cartilages (*cartilagines arythaenoideae).* They are both located on the cricoid cartilage (*cartilago cricoidea*), on which the thyroid also rests. All these cartilages can slide and tilt between each other. In this complicated arrangement, the vocal folds can open and close, tighten or relax, contract and give in, either in separate movements or as a combination of movements.

It is important to bear in mind that the primary function for the vocal folds is to close the windpipe and protect the lungs. There are five pairs of muscles inside the larynx. Only one of them, the Posticus (*musculus cricoarytaenoideus posterior)* opens the gap between the vocal folds, the glottis (*rima glottidis).* The closing effect from the other four muscle pairs is very strong and there is no reason what-soever to exercise the closing when the vocal folds have their healthy function. Only in states like vocal fold paralysis might it be needed.

The inner – intrinsic – laryngeal muscles are innervated by the 10th cranial nerve; *Nervus Vagus (CN X)*, which splits into two branches to the various muscles.

*

In the larynx vocal pitch, voice-register and intensity are controlled in a complex interaction between muscle activity and the air-pressure.

Our ability to voluntarily move the laryngeal muscles and the different cartilages independently of each other is limited. It is primarily with the aid of the air-flow that we activate and affect the laryngeal muscles in sound production. Some control is also done

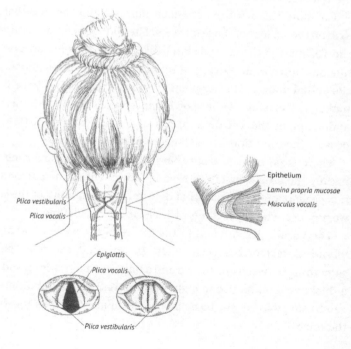

by how we adjust the vocal tract, our resonators. All this together with the position of neck and head indirectly affects the muscles inside larynx.

Trying to separate the specific functions of the individual laryngeal muscle-pairs is more for people in the academic field than for the vocal practitioner. In reality these muscles work together in a coordinated, harmonious and rhythmical mechanical system.

Vocal folds

The core of the vocal folds are the vocal muscles (*musculus vocalis*) also called Vocalis. These two muscles are surrounded by three layers of fibres and mucus membranes (*lamina propria mucosae*) together with a surface layer of epithelium. This relation between a firmer core surrounded by a looser cover is in voice science called 'Body-cover Theory.'

Compare this with the stomach muscles and the loose fat and skin on the surface of those muscles. The abdominal muscles are like the Vocalis and the fat and skin is like the mucous membrane. The mucous membrane surrounding the Vocalis moves more than the actual muscles during phonation. It waves around Vocalis and makes the closing of the glottis more efficient. It is the activity and shape of the Vocalis muscles together with the airflow that provide the condition for the mucous wave to appear.

There is no need to train the Vocalis muscle to be strong. It is mainly the efficiency of the closing movement of the surrounding mucosa, not of the muscle, that determines the quality of the sound we produce. The key factor for the closing is the airflow.

The Vocalis are situated in the centre of the larynx and are the vibrating part of the vocal folds. In an adult the folds can be something between one to two and a half centimetres long and have a thickness around five to eight millimetres. Individual differences can be tangible but the basic is that the longer the folds the deeper the voice.

Children have shorter vocal folds than adults. During adolescence the cartilages and the vocal folds start to grow, and we enter the voice break. With the increased length of the folds the voice becomes deeper. It is important to point out that this happens to both sexes. Some few can get stuck in their pre-adolescence voice and avoid releasing their voice down into the grown-up voice they should have. Later in life, during the menopause, there can come a second change in the voice. The voice might be deeper and hoarser, due to the dryness in the tissue that can occur. Don't worry about working with and using your voice during these times of change. If you work with your voice in the right way you will, with time, adjust to your physical changes.

*

Just above the vocal folds are the ventricular folds, sometimes called the false vocal folds (*plica vestibularis*). They are mucosal pleats in the laryngeal wall and they have no function in phonation except for sounds like growling in hard rock or throat singing. In the cavity between the vocal and ventricular folds there are mucous glands that provide lubrication for the vocal folds. If you experience more mucosa than usual in the throat after intensive voice work, it is these glands that lubricate the folds a bit extra. Usually, this is a sign that you have worked a bit too hard or failed to support your folds with the proper amount of airflow.

VOCAL FOLD VIBRATION
(MYOELASTIC-AERODYNAMIC THEORY)

The closing of the glottis during phonation comes mainly from the air pressure. We talk about three different pressures: the pressure below glottis (subglottal), the pressure inside glottis (transglottal), and the pressure above glottis (supraglottal). These three different air pressures affect each other and to some extent control the movements of the vocal folds.

The air pressure creates the rapid movements – vibrations – of the vocal folds. Each cycle of vibration has three phases:

1. Pre-setting
2. Aerodynamic separation
3. Returning together.

The vocal folds are softly closed [1] by the Vocalis muscles. The air pressure builds up under them (subglottis) and the vocal folds are blown apart [2] in a movement that is at the same time upwards and apart. The release of the air makes the air pressure under the vocal folds drop so that they are no longer pushed apart. When the air streams out between the folds (transglottis) the air creates a negative pressure that sucks them together. This, together with the inner elastic recoil of the folds' tissue, closes the glottis [3] again.[1]

Too many ideas concerning a need to train and control the closure of the glottis exist. The vocal folds are sucked together by the airflow streaming through the glottis, and the inner elastic recoil of the tissues. Nothing else is needed.

*

It is the amount of the cycles in the vocal folds that determines what pitch we produce. The average amount of vibrations in the female speaking voice is around 200 movements per second (200 Hz) and for the male around 100 movements (100 Hz). When we are singing a high note the vibrations of the vocal folds will be much faster. The soprano's high C is around 1046 Hz and the tenor's is half the amount at 523 Hz. Now, this says something about the amount and speed of the vibrations in the vocal folds.

*

---

1 When the air flows past a narrowing surface it creates a negative pressure. This phenomenon is called the Bernoulli effect.

The balance between the activity in the Vocalis and the subglottal pressure determines the intensity and amplitude of the voice.

Higher contraction of the Vocalis muscle makes the mucous membrane thicker, looser and more flexible. The thicker membrane together with the subglottal air-pressure prolongs the closing phase of the glottis and makes the folds' vibrating movement bigger. The prolonged closing phase and the bigger movements of the vocal folds is what increase the vocal intensity and the amplitude of the voice.

If the subglottic pressure becomes too high, if we push the air out, the vocal folds will not be able to close smoothly. It's rather like when a gentle stream turns wild after heavy rain and suddenly drags everything along with it. Especially in singing the voice can get unstable, a bit wobbly or flapping. On the other hand, if the subglottic pressure is too low the vocal folds will not have enough drive to be sucked together and the voice can be breathy or get creaky. The goal is, as always, to have a good balance between airflow and activity in Vocalis.

A good example is a flag: too little wind and the flag just hangs there limply whereas with too strong a wind the flag stands straight out and only the edge flaps wildly. It is not until the size and material of the flag are in good balance with the speed of the wind that the flag waves.

Try to discover this delicate balance yourself using these two exercises.

➤ Firstly, take a soft note and then increase the air pressure by abruptly pulling your stomach in. Did you notice what happened with the sound? Right at the beginning, before your vocal folds adjusted to the higher pressure, you probably got a harsh quality.

➤ Secondly, take a note again and this time quickly relax your stomach and notice what happens then. The sound probably disappears when the airflow goes down in intensity.

VOCAL REGISTERS

Registers are, simply put, different working modes for the vocal folds that result in changes in quality of the voice. The terminology around register is confusing. Various terminology is used both in the academic fields and in the different fields of vocal training.

To sort out the confusions around register we need to go back to the early era of voice training. Some schools seem to have spoken from a point of the physical sensations, where the sound could be experienced in the body, such as vibrations in the chest or the head. Other schools talked about the voice from an acoustic point of view; about the quality of the sound. Some of these traditions still live on in vocal training and can easily be confused with the scientific terminology.

During the sixteenth century different terminology was used. Giulio Caccini (1551–1618), one of the most influential composers and singing teachers of the time, talked about *Voce piena e naturale* (full and natural voice) versus *Voce finta* (false voice). In the beginning of what developed into the western opera of today, singers used these contrasting qualities between the dense strong 'natural' voice and the thinner softer 'false' voice. This play between these qualities in the voice was called chiaroscuro. The transition between these two registers should be done as inconspicuously as possible and was called *Ponticello* (small bridge). As time went by, the transition became an artistic element in itself. In the nineteenth century, the transition had become a register of its own: *Voix mixte.*[1]

*

Today voice science distinguishes between the laryngeal aspect, how the vocal folds move, and the acoustic aspect, how the voice sounds. Register is about the laryngeal aspect. The resonators' contributions, the placement, are irrelevant.

---

1 Named so by Manuel Garcia (1805–1906).

According to most definitions a register is defined by:

- a specific vibratory pattern in the vocal folds
- a certain range of pitches with
- almost identical quality of the sound

The main vocal registers are:

- falsetto or loft register
- modal (the usual speaking voice)
- vocal fry, pulse or creaking voice

There is a fourth register, the whistle or flageolet register. It is the highest register in pitch. Not all of us have that register and the physiology around it is the least understood of the registers.

Modal voice and falsetto are both registers that can be used in voice production. The vocal fry, or the creaking voice, is not a functional way of using the vocal folds. The airstream is too low and the folds have no chance to accomplish a proper vibration. Hence you can nearly hear every closing of the folds as a rattling sound. Speaking in vocal fry is tiring for the folds and should be avoided. If this has become a habit, try to increase your airstream and the fry will change to the modal voice which is a much healthier way of speaking.

Modal voice is when the Vocalis muscle contracts and becomes short and fat. The surrounding mucosa becomes loose and can freely wave around the Vocalis and create a good closing and opening of the glottis. The sound becomes full and strong. This is what in singing tradition is called chest voice – Caccini's *Voce piena e naturale*.

Falsetto is when the Vocalis is passively stretched out and becomes long and thin. The mucosa is less free and no proper wave occurs. The closing of the vocal folds becomes less efficient and the sounds become weaker and thinner. In singing tradition this is usually called head voice – Caccini's *Voce finta*.

Think of this relation between the vocal muscle and the surrounding mucosa as the relation between the stomach muscle and the belly fat. If you constrict your stomach muscles so you bend a little forward the fat and skin will be easier to move on the surface of the muscles – the modal voice. If you bend backwards your stomach muscles will be passively stretched and it will be more difficult to move the surface of skin and fat – the falsetto.

In most singing traditions there is also 'mix' or 'middle' voice. It is a voice that is in either falsetto or modal register, but is trained so that the vocal folds *function* more like the contrasting register. There is activity in the Vocalis muscle and the mucous membrane is free to wave around the muscle and the closing phase of the folds are more efficient. The voice is rich and full in quality but not as heavy as in chest voice nor as thin as in falsetto. As I understand it this is similar to *Voix mixte*.

When a male singer takes a high pitch with a very light and soft quality without going over into falsetto or when a female singer takes a low pitch with a heavy darker quality without going into the modal voice, this is how I see the mixed voice. They 'mix' the qualities between the modal and the falsetto register. This is also how modern countertenors have trained their voice. Their falsetto has a modal like function, rich and powerful in sound.

Some of the confusion around register might come from when one not separate the vibratory pattern in the vocal folds from the contribution of the vocal tract, i.e. the resonance. Head or chest resonance can be used regardless of what register one is singing in.

THE USE OF REGISTERS

During the sixteenth and seventeenth century the artistic aim was to have a blending of volume in singing; to sing just as strong on the high notes as on the low ones. However, the quality or character of the sounds between the high and low notes was contrasting. Seek out a recording with Fernando De Lucia (1860–1925) and listen to how he uses these contrasting qualities. *Ecco ridente* from Rossini's *Il Barbiere di Siviglia* (recorded 1904), is a brilliant example of this style and taste. One can easily hear how De Lucia uses the different registers as tools for the artistic expression. However, he keeps his voice pretty much in the same placement all the time.

Today in classical singing there is instead a blending of the sounds; the voice has an even timbre all through the range. The aim is to smooth out the sound differences both inside a register and in the transition between them, making the voice sound more or less the same from top to bottom. As a result of this blending most modern classical singers have much stronger high than low notes.

In all singing the change of register and sound quality is either hidden or used. In classical western singing there is a sound blending and in today's non-classical singing, such as musical singing, the contrasting timbre between registers are used as an artistic tool. In some cultures and genres the break in itself is used as an expression (yodelling is an example of this).

*

In the change of register different antagonistic muscle groups inside larynx, together with the air stream, adjust the vocal folds. Most times the muscle groups work smoothly together. In the transfer between the modal and falsetto voice a clear break can sometimes be heard. That happens when the antagonists 'jump' in for each other instead of 'sneaking' in and softly taking over. This is something that can be avoided with training.

Let us return to the explanation about antagonistic muscles, the biceps and the triceps in the upper arm: one muscle-group contracts while the other gives in (see p. 21). In the same way does the Vocalis muscle and its antagonistic muscles (*musculus cricothyreoideus*) interact. This cooperation between Vocalis and its antagonistic muscles together with the airstream controls register and pitch.

Being able to blend the different registers, and avoid the abrupt break, is like switching between bending and stretching the arm so smoothly that no one can see when the change of direction occurs: the antagonistic muscles cooperate smoothly. In voice this is something you mainly do with the help of the air flow and air pressure. You use the air to slide through the vocal registers. The transition between the different registers is called *passaggio*.

Within each register, we have small changes of vocal qualities and functions. We can compare it with the different gears in a car engine. When you drive and either increase or decrease your speed you need to change gear but it's still the same engine. This applies to the voice also. Within your range you suddenly come to notes that are less easy to hit, or the quality of your voice changes; then it is time to 'change gear.' We do this with help of the resonators and the subglottic air pressure – so that the vocal folds smoothly and easily can change their vibrational pattern.

*

From a singing point of view, all this doesn't really matter. If you base your voice work on the airflow, the vocal folds usually adjust to the quality you aim for. Don't pay too much attention to what kind of voice or register you are in. After all, it is the same vocal folds you use – regardless of register – so just sing and trust your body to handle it.

An image of the free and uninhibited voice can be a triangle with a broader and darker base and a slender and lighter top. Inside this triangle, the voice is free to move around without any dramatic breaks. This is possible if the airflow is always the source for the voice.

I would like to say that the focus on what happens inside the larynx comes from a fear of losing control. It blocks release of sounds and keeps the speaker or singer focused on the mechanical sound production instead of letting the sound production occur as a result of the body's response to the inner life of imagination, intentions and emotions.

VIBRATO

Vibrato can be described as a small regular change in pitch and intensity around the intended pitch. According to most studies, vibrato comes from the larynx and pharynx. A healthy vibrato occurs in well-coordinated balanced singing, based on the airstream. A free vibrato adds richness to the singing voice.

The extent of vibrato is highly individual. A free vibrato can be anything from a fast, flickering sound to something as big as a semi-tone. Vibrato should feel natural and comfortable to a singer and not come from tensions. I strongly advocate against creating a vibrato since this nearly always creates tensions. The free vibrato evolves by itself when the voice is free and released. The ageing voice can acquire a slow rocking vibrato, due to reduction of the elasticity in the tissues. A very fast small vibrato or a totally 'straight' tone can indicate tensions in the jaw, tongue or neck area.

TONGUE, PALATE AND JAW: SOME OF THE ARTICULATORS

The tongue's (*lingua,* or *glossa* in Greek) primary function is to shift the food in the mouth when we chew and swallow. It has an advanced structure that allows it to move in many different directions. The fibres go transversely (side to side), vertically (up–down) and longitudinally (back–front). The tongue is anchored on the top side of the hyoid bone, the jaw and in the bones behind the ears. It forms the floor of the oral cavity (*cavum oris*). The tongue is also the most important articulator. It is a tricky muscle that happily helps out with high notes and strong sounds. It shouldn't: the tongue must stay relaxed.

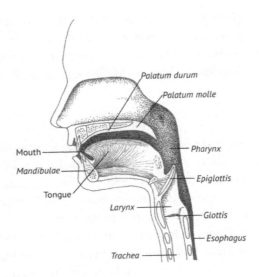

Explore your tongue.

> Firstly, place your finger on the soft part under your lower
> jaw, behind the jaw bone, and press the tip up against the
> floor of the mouth.

> Secondly, speak and notice how the rear part of your tongue
> moves when you articulate.

> Thirdly, tense your tongue and feel how it hardens against
> your finger. Relax and feel how soft it becomes.

> And finally, take a note and keep it, tense and relax your
> tongue and notice the different qualities of the sound.

On the bottom side of the hyoid bone hangs the larynx in its ligament. The back of the tongue affects the position of the larynx and the shape of the throat. A relaxed tongue opens the throat, releases the jaw and increases the volume of the oral cavity, something that benefits the resonance and the freedom of the vocal folds.

The palate's primary function is to prevent food from entering the cavity of the nose. While swallowing it is lifted as the tongue transports the food into the gullet. When we breathe with the mouth closed the soft palate (*palatum molle*) is lowered and the air enters via the nose. The soft palate meets the hard palate (*palatum durum*) in the middle of the oral cavity. The hard palate is made up of bone dressed in mucous membrane.

> ➤ Place your tongue behind the front teeth in the ceiling of your mouth and lick as far back as possible, or feel with your index finger. Push softly against the hard palate and gently slide back to where it turns soft. You will feel where the hard palate ends and the soft palate begins. At the end of the soft palate is the grape-shaped *uvula*. If you look in a mirror with your mouth wide open and your neck bent back, you might be able to see the *uvula*.

This area is of interest when we manipulate the quality of the sounds, and is part of the resonators. If we lower the soft palate too much when speaking or singing, the sound streams up in the nose cavity and becomes nasal and muffled.

The jaw's (*mandibulae*) primary function is to chew the food; we grind it between our teeth. The joint of the jaw (*art. temporo-mandibularis*) is placed on each side of the head, close to the ears. Both joints act simultaneously at jaw movements. The jaw can move sideways, down-up and forward-backward or in a rotary movement that combines these directions.

> ➤ Gently insert a finger – with the fingertip facing forward – in the ear canal. Now speak. Notice the movements of the joints of the jaw when you articulate.

We have four large chewing muscles which are attached either to the inside or the outside of the jaw and to the skull. Tensions in the chewing muscles are common and can have a negative influence on the voice.

> Open your mouth really wide and notice how the larynx is pressed down a little.

You can open your mouth without moving the lower jaw, by bending the head back; the upper jaw (*maxilla*) is part of the skull. Perhaps not the most efficient way of opening the mouth – and in voice production it easily closes the neck.

The tongue, the palate and the jaw together with the lips are the articulators. We use them to produce vowels and consonants. They are also crucial factors in creating resonance of the voice.

VOCAL RESONANCE

The laryngeal sound (or laryngeal note) – the sound that the vocal folds create – is not enough without its system of resonators. Compare the vocal tract, our sound-box, with how different rooms have different acoustics – the size and shape of a room affect the soundwaves and so do different surfaces. The soundwaves can either be enhanced or subdued.

We can create a huge variety of sounds by changing the shape of the vocal tract with the help of the tongue, jaw, lips, soft palate and the position of the head. This is called the 'Source-filter theory,' the sound from the vocal folds is the source and the vocal tract is the filter.

All tones have overtones. They are part of the acoustic spectrum that gives a sound its character. When we change the shape of our vocal tract we reinforce different overtones. Groups of overtones which are amplified by the vocal tract are called formants. It is by using these formants that we can create the different vowels and also make the voice more efficient.

> Intone a vowel and slide into another vowel without changing pitch. What you did was change the shape of your vocal tract, hence changing what groups of overtones that are strong.

> Try again by switching from one clear vowel to another vowel. While doing so take note of which of the articulators that move or change position.

> Hold a note and at the same time slowly open and close your mouth. Pay attention to how the changing size and shape of your mouth change the quality of the sound. Once again you changed the acoustic room – your vocal tract – and in that way manipulated the sound.

> Hold a note again, keep the pitch and move your head. Bend the head back, then bow your neck, all on one breath. Notice how the changing shape of the vocal tract affects the sound.

*

Finding the 'placing of the voice' in our vocal tract is about how to find the best acoustic shape for each pitch and sound. This is how the voice can be projected effortlessly into the auditorium. The western way of singing opera developed from small soft voices, that only needed to be heard over one or two instruments in smaller rooms, into the typical opera voices of today that need to be heard over an orchestra of more than a hundred instruments in a big opera house. It is by optimizing the overtones and formants that the voice can be heard over modern orchestras, or, as the Swedish opera singer Birgit Nilsson said: "The voice needs to have ping." With this she meant the focused resonance that makes it possible for the voice to surf above the sound carpet of the orchestra. The voice surfs over the orchestra with help of the overtones – it is not heard because it is very loud or strong. This 'surfing' goes for any kind of voice that needs to be heard in a big space; speaking or singing voice. They all need to have the 'ping.'

No less important is that a good placing of the voice releases the vocal folds from pressure and improves the acoustic energy and the longevity of the voice.

ACOUSTICS

Sound is small variations in the air pressure that occur very rapidly, one after the other. When we speak the vocal folds chop up the air into pulses. Each vocal fold cycle makes the molecules of the air bounce together or go apart – compressions and rarefactions – in an oscillating movement called *periodic sound waves.* The soundwaves move through the air like ripples on water.

When the molecules of the air oscillate back and forth, the molecular movement spreads from the source of the sound to the receiver of it. It reaches our eardrums and makes them vibrate. The brain interprets these vibrations as sounds. Furthermore, the soundwaves can also set other objects and materials in vibration. You have probably experienced this when all of your body starts to vibrate at certain pitches at a concert.

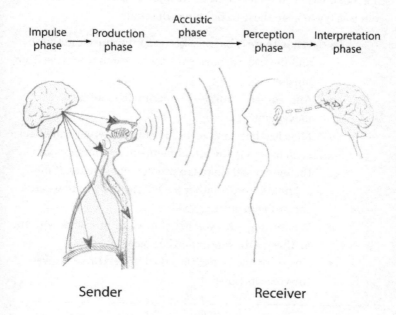

Impulse phase → Production phase — Accustic phase → Perception phase → Interpretation phase

Sender   Receiver

Sounds are distinguished from each other in four different ways:

- duration – time: in voice it is related to the airflow; how long time we produce a sound with an uninterrupted airflow;
- pitch – frequency (Hz): is related to the activity in the vocal folds;
- loudness – intensity (dB): is related to the subglottal pressure;
- quality of the sound: is related to the function of the vocal folds and how different overtones, harmonies, in the sound are amplified.

*

To make it easier to understand the principles behind the following exercises try to keep these basic things in mind.

- When there is balance between the muscle activity and the task we perform – then we can work free from tensions.
- Antagonistic muscles cooperate to stabilize a movement.
- Muscles that don't seem to belong together can affect each other via the attachments in common bones via the tendons. If there is a problem in a muscle it may originate from another part of the body than where the problem occurs.
- Whatever genres you use your voice in – work with the airflow as the motor for the voice.
- The resonance – not the effort in the throat – gives the voice its power.

All vocal exercises should have their base in the airflow.

Basic Voice Work

PREPARING THE BODY AND MIND

These basic exercises are the foundation for all development of a voice. If you would like to improve your vocal skill on a non-professional level they will most likely be enough. These exercises are also the base for the In-depth chapter.

First comes a long section about releasing and warming up the body. This part is crucial for voice work. Never jump directly into sound making – prepare your body and mind for the work. These exercises will also benefit all your wellbeing and give you a good awareness of your body and your breathing, which will hopefully reduce tensions both in body and mind.

Here are some important things to consider before any exercise.

- Voice work begins in the body, so pay attention to how your body feels – sense and experience your body. Remember that body and mind must work together.

- It is unwise to monitor your voice by listening to how you sound. If you listen to your voice rather than feel it in your body, you might easily be fooled by the different acoustics of different rooms. Sometimes the acoustics benefit sound, sometimes it don't. The physical sensation is a far more reliable way of checking your voice. If your voice and body feel right then trust in that.

- Another aspect is that our *inside* voice (the sound we hear internally) is different from our *outside* voice (what others hear). This is because the vibrations from our voice are transmitted inside the body through the bones to our ears, as well as by the air.

- Pay attention to your body, your breathing and your mind both before and after an exercise. Compare. What happened? Did things get better or worse?

- If you get stuck on an exercise, or it seems like it isn't working smoothly, go back to the step in the exercise where things worked and try again. Don't forget that the obstacles might be in the mind as well as in the body.

- Resist the temptation to evaluate or control your work during the exercise.

- Don't stop or inhibit any movements or emotions. Remember: breathing is also a movement.

- You can only do one thing at a time. Don't try to get everything right from the beginning. *Festina lente* as the ancient Romans said: hasten slowly.

- Let the effects and responses occur naturally – don't strive for them.

- Be aware of any exercises that cause pain. What sort of pain is it? Is it a good kind of pain that might benefit the body or is it a bad kind of pain that feels as though it is causing damage? If the latter adjust the exercise or stop doing it.

- Rest for a while if your voice gets tired. Have some water. Assess what it was that caused the tiredness.

- Exercise and repetition is the mother of success. The challenge is to keep working even when you feel that you have done it to the limit of boredom. When that happens find new challenges in the same old exercises. Keep digging and exploring, but if you get tired or lose focus, take a break. Work with quality – not quantity.

- Remember that what feels unnatural might only be unusual for you. Our habits can easily fool us to confuse these two.

- Working with voice takes a huge amount of energy, mentally and physically. Energy should not be confused with effort, tension or stress.

- During the work, tune into the small sensations – voice work is not big muscles doing big things.

- The purpose of the exercise is more important than exactly how it is performed.

- You must be mentally present in the exercise. If you perform the exercise mechanically or in a routine way it will never produce the same results as when the mind is engaged. Body and mind must work together. After all we are a unit of body and mind.

- Never work with or warm up body, breathing or voice randomly or in a routine way. Pay attention to your daily status – and put the effort in where it is needed. Most importantly: do not evaluate your findings, just say 'hello, how are we today?' to your body. Pay attention, notice, and attune yourself to small sensations or changes in your body or mind.

- Fear of failure is a poison to creativity and development. Relax and allow yourself to have fun.

Finally, before you begin any exercise always read it through a couple of times so you've grasped the idea. It is better to work fluidly rather than keep referring back to the book.

RELAX – RELEASE

In Swedish, we have the two excellent words *avslappnad* and *avspänd*. They might seem nearly the same but there is an ocean between them. The different meanings are very important in body and voice work. *Avslappnad* is the word for relaxed in a passive way; like the moment before you fall asleep. *Avspänd* is when you work with the appropriate muscle activity needed for the task: active but free from tensions.

Standing still or sprinting are two activities that demand different levels of activity. However, they can both be done with adequate amounts of energy, free from unnecessary muscle tension or stress. This is how you need to work with voice; with activity in mind and body but still without tensions and stress. In this condition, you are ready to act and react.

Voice work should always be carried out with an adequate amount of energy for the task. The goal with the upcoming exercises is to find a freedom in the body so that you – even under high stress and excitement – can keep your breathing free and flexible. In this way the voice can stay totally free. You can experience the nervousness and at the same time learn not to let it lock your body or mind.

Keep in mind that the muscles function as antagonists. There will not be any locked or tensed joints when the antagonists are in good balance with each other.

SCANNING AND EXPLORING YOUR BODY

This is an exercise which allows you to explore and pay attention to your body: a scanning. It will let you know what state your body is in today and what you need to focus on in the following of body, breathing and voice warm-up.

➤ Pay attention to how you are standing on the floor and how your feet feel against the floor.

➢ Gently shift your body's weight from your left to right foot a couple of times. Come to a stop when you find stability in the middle and the weight is evenly spread between the feet.

➢ Gently shift your weight from the heels to the toes, back and forth. Come to a rest with the same amount of weight across your feet.

● Adjust a little, so that there is a tiny bit more weight on the front of your feet. Feel the activity in the toes. Ensure your foot's entire sole is in contact with the floor.

➢ Pay attention to your knees:

● how do they feel?
● tense the front of your thighs. What happened to the knee-cap?
● release your thighs again and let the knee-cap fall down. This is 'free and open' knees.

➤ Focus on your lower and middle back and place a hand firmly there – how do the muscles feel?

- Tense your thighs again so that the knee-cap slides up.
- Did this affect the muscles in the lower and middle back?
- Release the thighs and the knees – what happened to your back now?

➤ Focus on the lower part of your abdomen, from belly-button to the groin.

- Can you relax in this area?
- Move your weight to your heels.
- How did this shift affect the area of your lower abdomen?
- Return to having the weight more on the front and the toes.
- What happened now?

➤ Bend over, with soft knees, so that your head and arms hang relaxed towards the floor.

- Roll up the spine vertebrae by vertebrae. Start in the lower back, as if you pulled the tail (i.e. tailbone) between your legs, like a sad dog.
- Let your shoulders fall into place.
- Finally roll your neck and head up, so that you gaze toward the horizon.
- Where did your shoulders end up? If necessary lift them slightly and then drop them.

➤ Feel how your head is floating lightly at the top of the neck, like a buoy on the sea, and ensure that it can move freely.

➤ Let the jaw hang free and relaxed with a small gap between the teeth. The lips can still be closed.

➤ Let your tongue rest on the floor of the mouth.

➤ Have you lost your equilibrium? If so – find your way back to it.

➤ Where in the body is the breathing?

➤ How do your lower abdomen, lower back and chest feel? Tensed or relaxed?

➤ Can the air come and go freely?

➤ Tighten your toes. How does that affect the rest of your body and your breathing? Release the toes. Compare.

➤ Continue the same way with tightening/releasing and comparing, upward through the body: knees, buttocks, abdominal muscles, lower back, shoulders, neck, and finally the jaw.

➤ Keep your knees open, free and soft throughout.

➤ Finally, now when you hopefully are balanced and free from tensions: Pay attention to where you have your pelvic floor, i.e. the area between the anus and the groin. Are you tensed or relaxed here? Squeeze the muscles in this area and then relax.

SCANNING WHILE WALKING

Here is an alternative scanning exercise. It requires a fair bit of space so it might be worth taking the opportunity to do this exercise when you are out for a walk. Don't forget to explore the body without valuating your findings.

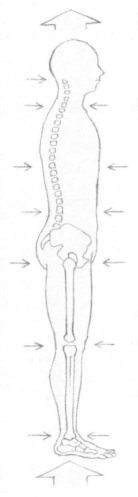

> ➤ Walk around while you step by step scan through your body. Spend at least one minute on every step; pay attention and try to experience your body.

Feet and legs

> ➤ Focus on your feet and pay attention to how they feel against the floor:

- which part of the foot first makes contact with the floor?
- what part comes next?
- what part of the front foot sole meets the floor first?
- which toe meets the floor first?
- which toe leaves the floor last?
- notice how your feet meet the floor and roll over, from heel to toe, during a step.

> ➤ Now focus on your ankles:

- how do they feel?
- smooth or not?
- compare the right and the left ankle. Do they feel the same or different?
- can you notice the cooperation between the movement of your feet and the movement in your ankles?

➤ Next are your knees:

- how do they feel?
- smooth or not?
- compare the right and the left knee.
- can you notice the cooperation between the movement of your feet, your ankles and the movement in your knees?

➤ And now focus on your hip joints:

- how do they feel?
- smooth or not?
- compare the right and the left joint.
- can you notice the cooperation between the movement of your feet, your ankles, your knees and the movement in your hips?

➤ Alter your speed – move faster or slower – and pay attention to how this affects the movement in your feet, ankles, knees and hips. Does the cooperation between them change as well?

➤ Now walk in a different way – more on the outside or inside of your feet and then more on the heels or more on the toes – noticing as you do so the changes that occur in your body.

➤ And now resume some comfortable walking.

Pelvis

➤ Now pay attention to your pelvis:

- how does it move? Is it rocking from side to side, or is there more of a screwing movement, or is it completely still and locked? Or...?
- can you feel that the movement of the hips is a prolonging of the movement of the legs in walking?

Torso and spine

➢ Focus on both the lower part of your abdomen and your back (i.e. from groin to just below the bellybutton, and from the tailbone up to the same height):

- how is the balance between the front and the back?
- can you notice the cooperation between your pelvis and this part?
- any tensions?
- do you have any movement from the breathing down here?

➢ Focus on the part from the bellybutton up to the diaphragm (solar plexus) and on the same height in your back:

- how is the balance between front and back?
- how is the cooperation with the lower part?
- any tensions?
- any breathing movements?

➢ The sternum and the back:

- how is the balance between front and back?
- any parts pushed forward or pulled back?
- any slumping or collapsing?
- any movements from the breathing?
- how is the cooperation with the lower part?

The top of the spine

➢ The neck and head:

- notice how the head balances on the top section of the spine.
- how is the balance between front and back?

- is the head dropping or pulled back?
- is the jaw clenched or free? (If it's hard to judge, try biting down and then release.)

Finally

➢ Return to the focus on your feet. See if you can find the connection from the sole of your feet through the ankles – knees – hips – pelvis – lowest part of your spine – the abdomen area – the thoracic area – the neck and all the way up to the top of the skull. Ideally the whole body is connected. The posture is neither slumped together nor hoisted or stretched up. It is balanced, hence free to move and breathe.

➢ If you are outdoors pay attention to how different grounds affect your body. Does walking uphill or downhill change anything?

➢ Try the exercise wearing different shoes as well. It is important, and possible, to be able to find a freedom in ankles, knees, hips and spine even when in high heels.

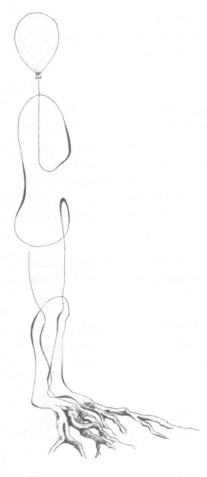

Your body's centre of gravity needs to be low. Always try to use your feet and legs as the source for energy. A surprising amount of vocal difficulties stem from locked knees, which inhibits full breathing. Imagine yourself as having rooted feet, a floating head and nothing in between.

With the awareness of your body that you have now, let's move into the next section: to open and release the body.

FROM SCANNING TO RELEASING

After scanning the body it is time to adjust and change the parts that we discovered to be in need of attention. A scan makes the subsequent releasing work more efficient; we can spend time and focus on the parts that need it – instead of working in an unspecific or generalised way. You can also go back and do a new scan after the releasing to see whether it made a difference.

Keep in mind that releasing exercises are just that, a release, not a workout, so work softly and gently. If you experience a crunching feeling during the upcoming exercises don't be alarmed. It might even be a little painful and if so, work slowly through that area and see if you can reduce the pain and improve the blood circulation.

Keep the exercise going even when it starts to be a bit demanding. Let the muscle work and be tired; a tired muscle relaxes much easier. Keep in mind the difference between 'good' pain and 'bad' pain. Adjust to, and respect, the 'bad' pain.

RELEASE OF HIP JOINTS AND KNEES

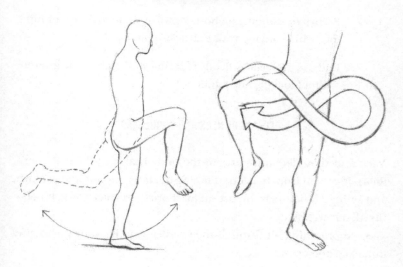

Start by releasing the joints of your hips and knees. If they are free from tensions this will help you with the free deep breathing in lower stomach and pelvic floor.

> ➤ Stand on one leg with the knee free and flexible.

> ➤ Gently swing the other leg back and forward in a pendulum movement.

> > • Keep the knee of the swinging leg relaxed and let the knee bend when the leg is up and in front of you. Swing the leg back and forward and try to keep both knee and hip smooth and flexible.

> ➤ Thereafter lift the leg and move the knee in the shape of an infinity sign (a horizontal eight) in front of you. Make sure you work from the hip joint.

> ➤ Change leg every now and then. Compare right with left hip joint.

> ➤ Return to standing on both legs. Continue to free your hip joints by swinging your buttocks a bit.

> ➤ End the exercise by firmly planting your feet on the ground without locking any joints.

RELEASE OF NECK AND SHOULDERS

Neck and shoulders are parts of the body that we all easily tense. Releasing them from tensions, making the muscles soft and smooth, and 'oiling' the joints is important for more than voice work. It benefits all our wellbeing.

Keep breathing all through the exercise and let your knees stay unlocked and open.

> ➤ Start by gently lifting your shoulders up to your ears and immediately drop them again. As they drop down, don't interfere with their final resting position. Do this about five to ten times and pay attention to where they come to rest. Are the right and left shoulders at the same height and position?

> ➤ Lift your shoulders again, keep them up by your ears and gently move them forwards and backwards slightly. Compare them with each other. Drop them and compare again.

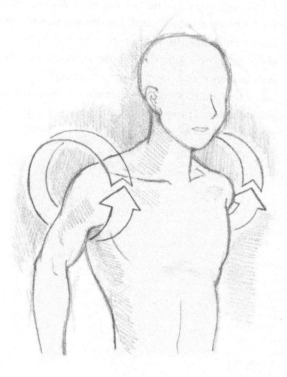

➤ Lift the shoulders and slowly let them go back and down in a wide circle, continue down and slowly circle forward upward. Make sure the movements start in the sockets and that the arms just hang there. Work in a wide circle so that the movements are felt all the way up in the neck. Continue until you feel a little tired, and then change direction. Finally lift and drop the shoulders.

> Gently swing your arms as if you are walking; one arm forward and one backward. Let the movement start in your hands and allow the swing continue all the way up to your shoulder blades. Keep the elbows released. Let the swing continue into a full circle, one arm going forward and the other backward. Shift direction after a couple of minutes of full swinging. The weight of your arms will release the muscles in the shoulders.

> Let your whole body be engaged in the exercises!

> Thereafter gently lift your shoulders a couple of times. Play around with both shoulders or just one shoulder and:

- compare fully lifted with half way lifted;
- compare half dropped down with fully dropped;
- finish with a full lift and drop the shoulders fully.

> Come to a rest. End with gently lifting and dropping your shoulders. Pay attention to if you feel any difference from before doing the exercise.

STRETCH EXERCISES FOR THE BREATHING – WITH HELP OF THE BREATHING

The voice can only reach its full potential if its basic motor is the breathing. It is therefore important that the body is free from tensions and stays flexible and soft. This exercise aims for an unobstructed, deep and calm breathing that can adapt to the vocal demands. In this exercise we use the breathing as part of the stretching, like a massage from the inside. It is not a breathing related to sound making.

All through the exercise direct big inhalations to the expanded area. Take your time with the inhalation and let it open up your body.

> ➤ Stand with your body balanced and centred.

> ➤ Clasp your hands behind your back with your thumbs toward the buttocks. Lift your arms out straight-up, keep your shoulder blades down (avoid tensions in your neck) and feel the stretch across your chest. Breathe actively high up in your chest six to eight times and expand this area with your inhalation. Release your arms and pay attention to any difference before and after. It is the breathing that will do the stretching, so don't push the chest out.

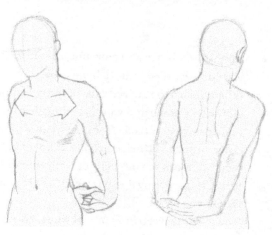

➤ Stretch your arms above your head, cross them and clasp your hands. Push your hands gently towards the ceiling so that the sides of your torso stretch. Take a big breath and let the inhalation expand and stretch the sides of your ribcage. Repeat six to eight times. Thereafter bend a little to the right side and breathe into your left side, and vice versa. Notice any difference between the sides.

➤ Hug yourself and bend gently forward with a relaxed neck and free knees. Feel the stretch between the shoulder blades; direct your inhalation to this area. Let the inhalation stretch and open your back.

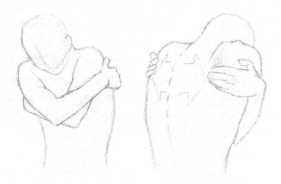

● Keep the embrace and continue, step by step, vertebrae by vertebrae, to bend over. Direct the inhalation to the curved area of the back until you are all the way down and your breathing has expanded and opened your back; from the shoulder blades, down to your buttocks. Keep your knees open, and bend your legs so you really can curve your back.

● When you are fully down release the arms, and let them hang down.

● Slowly roll up vertebrae by vertebrae, keep the breathing connected to the back.

This exercise above mainly expands the width of the back. In the exercise that follows we also expand the length of the back. You might find it a little uncomfortable at the beginning. Work gently and focus your breathing into the back's sore spots. Stay there for a moment and let the breathing massage your muscles from the inside.

The first step, stretching the top of your neck, is an isometric exercise. An isometric exercise is when the muscle is still but activated, when we tense the muscle without changing the length or position of it. The activity makes it easier to relax that muscle thereafter.

> Clasp your hands and place them on the back of your head.

- Begin by pushing the back of your head against your hands. Keep the hands firm so that the head can't bend or move backwards. Push backwards against your hands and then relax and slightly tilt your head down, so that the neck muscles in the base of your skull stretch a bit. In this position push the head against your hands again. Relax and tilt one more step downward. Press and relax until the chin is against your larynx and the nape of your head stretched upwards. Think of it as if each press/release is a cog moving down in a cog wheel. Don't pull your head down, it is enough with the weight of your hands.

> Thereafter:

- slowly roll down vertebrae by vertebrae. Curl up with the head 'in the middle' of the curve;

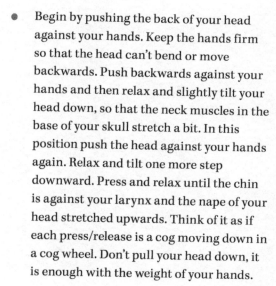

- breathe actively in your back, feel how your breathing expands and stretches the muscles;
- make sure your knees stay open;
- when you are fully down, let head, neck, shoulders and arms hang relaxed.

➢ Hang on down there and clasp your hands somewhere behind your thighs or knees. Push up your back like an angry cat, with its hackles raised and let the shoulder blades slide apart. Take a few active breaths, direct them to the extended spine. Release the arms and . . .

➢ sink into a squat, feel the stretch in the lower back and breathe in there. Keep your neck soft. Breathe calmly. Feel the breath gently stretch all the way down into your pelvic floor.

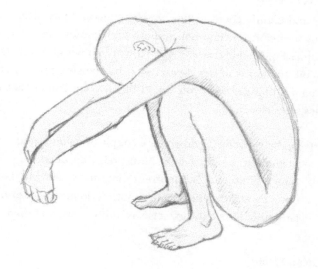

➤ Slowly stretch your legs, direct your buttocks and pelvis to the ceiling. Your upper body is still bent down in the direction to the floor. Take a few relaxed and deep breaths and slowly roll back up, vertebrae by vertebrae, beginning with the tailbone.

- When you are fully up, aim for the feeling that the head floats easily on top of the spine.
- Where did your shoulders end up? If they feel uncomfortable, lift and then drop them.

WARM UP AND RELEASE YOUR JAW, TONGUE AND FACE

After you have rolled up from the last exercise, finishing with a balanced body and neck, it's time to pay attention to the jaw, tongue and face.

Chewing muscles

Gently and calmly chew, rather big chewing, and pay attention to how the joints of your jaw feel. Smooth and comfortable? Any non-smoothness in the movement? Any pain? Keep working slowly and gently 'oil' the joints of the jaw to relax the chewing muscles. Keep chewing a bit longer than you would like to. Remember that tired muscles relax easier.

> ➤ Go between biting down for a couple of seconds and opening your mouth fully: biting, relaxing, opening, relaxing, biting. It is important that the transition between opening and closing of your mouth is done relaxed and smoothly. Finish the exercise by biting down and then relax.

Tongue and face

This exercise can cause pain in unexpected places – remember where the tongue is connected. Work with a relaxed neck all through the exercise.

> ➤ Place the tip of the tongue on the outside of your front teeth (behind your lips) in the upper jaw. Lick, with the tip of your tongue, the outside of the gum in a full circle. Pay attention to the transition between the upper and lower jaw, lick towards the inside of your ear.
>
> ● Repeat four to six times clockwise and counter-clockwise.
> ● Breathe calmly and keep your neck free during the exercise.
> ● Let the jaw and tongue rest relaxed.

➤ Place the tip of the tongue behind the lower front teeth and
bend the tongue out of your mouth. In this way, you gently
stretch the base of the tongue.

➤ Do some facial gymnastics; make big grimaces and wake up
all the small muscles of your face. Don't forget your lips,
they are an important part of the articulation. Move them
around and finish with a fluttering of your lips, like a
snorting horse, to relax them. Then, let the entire face hang
relaxed. All through the exercise, keep the shoulders and
hands relaxed and breathe calmly.

➤ Aim again for the feeling that the head floats easily on top
of the spine and that the jaw is relaxed.

By now you have scanned through your body and paid attention to
your shape of the day. You have released the shoulders and neck, the
rib cage and back, the jaw and tongue. Now it's time to wake up the
active breathing for voice.

Additional Exercises

The upcoming exercises are good to know, but is not part of a daily routine.

RELAX ON THE FLOOR

There will be days when you feel more like a piece of wood than a smooth and flexible human being, days when it is less easy to release your body or to find the deep and free breathing. Then it can be time for a proper relaxing on the floor. Try to find a place where you won't be disturbed.

➤ Lie down on the floor and put your legs up on a chair, with your knees at a ninety-degree angle. If necessary, add a thin book or something similar under your head to relieve your neck.

➤ Let the breath take care of itself. Imagine the air coming and going as a wave that gently rolls up on the beach and then rolls back into the sea. This is how the air streams in and out of your body.

➤ Pay attention to your spine. Feel the length of the spine against the floor, up through the neck and out through the crown. Don't forget to pay attention to the width of your back.

➤ Let the body give in with each new exhalation so that it becomes a little softer and a little more relaxed.

> Relax the jaw.

> Relax the facial muscles.

> Gently roll your head from side to side and feel that the neck and the jaw are free.

> Remain in this relaxed and open state for as long as required.

Always take your time as you get up after working on the floor. Never jump up or jerk yourself up. Try to keep the freedom and awareness from the relaxation on the floor. Make sure you bring this with you into standing.

> On your way up pay attention to your breathing, let the air come and go freely. Notice if you inhibit your breathing at any moment – if that happens, relax and come back to the free breathing.

   • If you are on your back, gently roll over to your side, your stomach and come up on your hands and knees.
   • Raise your buttocks in the air and slowly roll up vertebrae by vertebrae.
   • Make sure your breathing is uninhibited.

> Once you are up let your shoulders fall into position. Find the 'lightness' of your head and make sure your jaw hangs freely.

> Pay attention to where you have the weight on your feet – find your balance on both feet and a little bit more on the front part of the feet. Keep your knees free.

> Look out into a distant spot at eye-level.

EXTRA EXERCISES FOR JAW AND NECK

The muscles around the jaw, neck and tongue are intertwined and it can be tricky to find out where the root of tensions is. In voice work, I often think of this area as a unit.

The jaw

Here comes an isometric exercise for the jaw that is good to have in your tool-box: if your jaw is reluctant to relax with help of the softer releasing exercises.

Use the hand to fixate the jaw and inhibit the movements. Activate the different muscles of the jaw and 'push' the jaw in different directions against the blocking hand. Work softly, a firm push is more than enough. The jaw can move: up-down, to the sides and forward-backward. When chewing we combine this into a circular movement.

Opening the jaw:

> ➤ Place your fist under the jaw. Push up the fist a little against your jaw so that the jaw can't move, and at the same time try to open your mouth. Hold this activated phase for about three seconds.

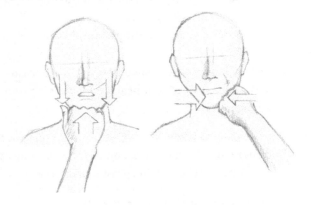

➢ Relax. Make sure you really relax, take the time needed to release the activated muscles.

➢ Repeat three times.

To the sides:

➢ This time place your right fist against the right side of your jaw. Push the jaw against your fist. Hold the jaw still with your hand and at the same time activate your muscles in the jaw for around three seconds.

➢ Relax and repeat three times. Take your time to relax between each activation.

➢ Change to the left side. Put your left fist against the jaw and activate your muscles.

➢ Relax and repeat three times.

Moving the jaw forward:

➢ Place your hand around the jaw, fixating it. Push the jaw out and work against the resistance of the hand.

➢ Relax and repeat.

Closing the mouth, biting together:

➢ Open your mouth and place some fingers on the front teeth in the lower jaw. Hold the jaw open, fixating it with your fingers. No violence please. Do not pull the jaw, just fixate it.

➢ Close you lower jaw against the fixating fingers in a mouth-closing movement, i.e. bite down without moving the jaw.

➤ Relax and release the jaw. Do not pull the jaw when you relax!

➤ Repeat.

Release your shoulders

The purpose of this exercise is to further release and relax your shoulders.

➤ Lie on your back, straight or bent legs depending upon what you find most comfortable. Relax there for a while. If you feel that the angle in your neck is uncomfortable put a thin book under your head.

- ➤ Put your arms straight up towards the ceiling. Keep elbows and hands free from tensions.

- ➤ Stretch your arms against the ceiling. Involve both the shoulder and shoulder blade and stretch until your shoulder blade leaves the floor.

- ➤ Thereafter relax and let the shoulder blades fall back on the floor. Really drop them back. Keep your arms in an upward position.

- ➤ You can work with both shoulders at the same time or one at a time. Compare the left with the right side.

- ➤ Repeat until you feel that your shoulders are more relaxed.

Stretching the front of the neck

Sometimes a stretch of the front of the neck is needed. Compensatory activity in the muscles in this area might sneak in as tensions, especially if you don't have a proper amount of airflow and support in your voice work.

- ➤ Stand up and gently bend your head back so your nose points towards the ceiling. 'Drop' your head back and relax. Keep it comfortable.

- ➤ In this position bring your jaw forward into an underbite. This will increase the stretch of the front neck muscles. Keep stretching for five to ten seconds.

- ➤ Relax your jaw and roll you head back up.

- ➤ Finally wriggle your head a little and come back to a centred and balanced position.

OPEN THE BACK

The back has important and strong muscles for the voice support. When the softer abdomen support is insufficient, the back must step in. This also goes for the situation when you need to sing and dance at the same time. Then your stomach is probably busy stabilizing for the dancing and the back needs to be more active in the support work.

If you feel that you need to work more on the opening of the back, try a backward somersault. It opens the back and makes it accessible for breathing.

> ➢ Lie on your back; roll over into a backward somersault. Stop in the middle with your knees hanging at the sides of your ears and your buttocks towards the ceiling. Relax and breathe into your back. The breathing will probably feel a bit uncomfortable since your larynx will be slightly squeezed. Try to keep your neck and shoulders relaxed though.

➤ Change between relaxed legs and stretched out legs.
This will open your back in different areas. Breathe into
your back and use the inhalation to open up. Hang there
for a couple of minutes.

➤ Slowly roll down, vertebrae by vertebrae, until your whole
back is on the floor.

➤ Stay in this position with your legs bent and the knees
tucked to your chest. Hug your knees and gently pull them
towards your chest. Keep directing your breathing towards
your back.

➤ Slowly place your feet on the floor with bent legs. Relax
there and breathe into your back.

➤ Come up into squat sitting. Breathe and expand your back.

➤ Raise your buttocks against the ceiling and from there
slowly roll up, vertebrae by vertebrae, until you are standing
balanced.

➤ Keep the breathing in the lower part of your back.

➤ See if you can find a breathing movement that connects
this lower part of the back with the lower part of the
abdomen.

➤ As always – let your head float freely on the top of the spine.
Free knees!

Basic Voice Work

BREATHING AND SOUNDS

Breathing is part of the body's autonomic system, which means that it is not primarily wilfully controlled. We usually don't think about our breathing, except when it is inhibited by one reason or another. All voice work starts with the breathing. It is the air that drives the vocal folds, nothing else. In the upcoming exercises the voiceless sounds [f] and [s] and the voiced sounds [v] and [z] will be used a lot. They are good to practice on. There is a slight resistance in the mouth for the airstream in these sounds, something that stimulates the activity of the exhalation/supporting muscles.

In all exercises the ≈ symbolizes the continuous airflow that connects sounds. Work with legato, keep the airstream in a continuous flow. It should be one continuous exhalation with small accents, a kind of stronger-weaker-stronger-weaker ongoing air flow. Avoid ending up in staccato with an interrupted airflow as ff. ff. ff. ff. It should be ff ≈ ff ≈ ff.

THE RELATION BETWEEN EXHALATION AND INHALATION

This exercise is designed to develop your awareness of the relation between your exhalation and inhalation. During the exercise just pay attention to your breathing instead of controlling it.

> ➤ Lie on your back on the floor. Find a relaxed quiet breathing.

➤ Notice where you feel movements from the quiet breathing in your body in different positions: lying on your back, bent legs, stretched legs, on your sides, on your stomach, and then in standing.

➤ Pay attention to:

- how deep does the breathing reach?
- do you breathe in the stomach and/or chest?
- does your midriff move or not?
- do you notice any breathing movements anywhere else in your body?
- did you discover any differences in the different positions?

➤ Choose the position that felt most benefitting for your relaxed breathing.

➤ Take a minute to adjust your breathing into a relaxed non-interfering breathing.

➤ Make the relaxed exhalation on an [f] or [s] sound. Keep your abdomen and diaphragm free from tensions.

➤ Extend the exhalation a little, then release. Let the inhalation take care of itself. Your body will take the needed quantity of air so *never force the inhalation.*

- Examine different lengths of exhalation.
- Do not interfere with the inhalation. Only pay attention to how it changes depending on the lengths of the exhalation.
- Try this in the different positions. Pay attention so that the neck and jaw remain relaxed.
- Extend the exhalation phase further by affecting the airflow through soft accents: 'ff ≈ ff ≈ ff ≈ ff ≈...' Explore different phrase lengths. Always let the inhalation take care of itself.

> ➤ Feel how the muscle activity increases with prolonged phrases and how this affects the airflow. Also notice how soft the activity can be.

> ➤ Maintain awareness of the height and width of your back and neck when you relax for the inhalation.

> ➤ How did the inhalation change with the different phrase lengths?

THE SUPPORTING MUSCLES IN THE LOWER ABDOMEN

The lower abdominal muscles, the muscles above your pubic bone (*pubis*), are central in voice production. Here follow three versions on how to find them. Try all three and pick the one that fits you best.

First version: lift your legs

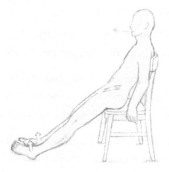

Sit on the edge of a chair with straight legs. Lean against the backrest. This exercise is easier to do without shoes.

> ➤ Notice the weight of the heels against the floor. Ease the pressure on the heels from the floor by lifting the legs a tiny bit. It is not a stretching exercise so there is no need to struggle with how straight your legs are.

➢ Relax.

➢ Repeat, and this time lift the heels some centimetres above the floor.

➢ Pay attention to the muscles above the pubic bone.

➢ Lift your legs again and notice the activity in these muscles in the absolute start of the movement. This is also the starting point for phonation.

➢ Make an [s] or [f] sound at the same time as you lift the legs.

● Let the start of the lifting and the start of the sound be simultaneous. Try to find the connection between them. You use the same stomach muscles. The start of the sound making is also the start of the leg lifting. Try to experience how this is one connected activity: 'sound and leg lifting.'

➢ Finish the sound and relax your legs at the same time and thus the abdominal muscles. The inhalation will then come spontaneously.

● This isn't a gym exercise. Lifting your legs a little is enough; even just releasing the pressure between the heels and the floor is enough.

➢ Try the exercise again. This time make it into a two-step lift of the legs and two flows of the sound 'ss ≈ ss'. Relax your legs and inhale.

➢ When you feel sure about finding the muscles above the pubis, make the sounds while standing.

● Can you still find the activity in the muscles in the pubic area on the [s] and [f]?

> ➤ Try it again. This time go from voiceless to voicing sounds in one exhalation. Take an [f] and gradually transit to a [v] and pay attention to what happens in the lower abdominal area during the transition from voiceless to voicing. Do the same thing with an [s] to a [z].

Second version: rock on your seat bones

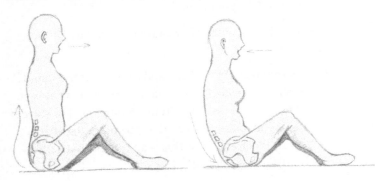

This next exercise is best done on the floor, but you can also try it while sitting on a hard chair. If you sit on a chair place your feet firmly on the floor so you have your legs at a ninety degree angle. Make sure that you have a three-point stability – foot, foot and buttocks – and keep free from the backrest.

> ➤ Sit on the floor with the legs slightly bent in front of you. Try to find your seat bones (*os ischia*) and sit on them.

> ➤ Move slightly so you sit behind the seat bones. You will slouch a little with your torso in this position.

> ➤ Move up on the seat bones again. The crown of the head strives towards the ceiling.

In this movement, when you return up on the seat bones, you activate the deeper abdominal muscles and part of the pelvic floor muscles. These are muscles highly involved in voice production.

> Move back behind the seat bones again.

> Go back up on them on a prolonged [f] sound, 'ffff'.

> The movement is 'up on' the seat bones so pay attention in case you end up in front of them. When you sit on the bones, picture the movement as continuing up towards the ceiling. This up going movement continues throughout the exhalation or sound making.

> With next inhalation drop behind the seat bones again. The movement and the inhalation are done simultaneously.

Try this 'up on the seat bone' throughout any kind of exhalation or sound making. The longer the phrase the slower the movement must be. Make sure that the sound making begins with the start of the 'going up on the bones' movement. The movement finishes with the end of the phrase. The motor for the sound and the motor for the movement are the same muscles. This is a good exercise to remember and bring into the in-depth section.

Third version: prolong the exhalation with voice

Use the following exercise to discover the supporting muscles in a different way. You can stand up, sit or lie down. Or, you can try all three positions. Compare how the different positions affect your breathing.

Usually, we inhale and then we speak: in this exercise we start to speak directly after the exhalation.

> ➤ Start in your relaxed breathing.

> ➤ In the end of a relaxed *exhalation* count aloud to five. Exhale and then count (no sipping of air before you start to count!).

> ➤ Release and let the inhalation be undisturbed.

> ➤ Exhale and see if you can count to ten without tensing up.

Did you notice that your abdominal muscles were more activated when there was less amount of air in the lungs?

This is an exercise to find and discover the breathing muscles. It is not a way to work with voice in speaking or singing. However, you will notice that there is a lot of air left in your lungs even after a relaxed exhalation – something that is good to have in mind later on.

THE INHALATION AREA

Now that you have discovered the muscles of the lower abdomen it is time to put them into action regarding breathing and voice.

All inhalations have to start in the abdominal wall below the belly button. The more demands your voice will meet the deeper and more active your inhaling needs to be. Release and relax your muscles from the belly button to the pubic bone and the pelvic floor – and let the relaxation go from there all the way up to the lower part of your back. During an inhalation you relax and open up this part with the feeling that the air can fall or dive right into your pelvic floor. From there, the air rises upward. If you suck in the air you will create tensions, so avoid that.

Take your time when you start to explore this area. Most of us avoid giving in as much as is needed. The stomach is a vulnerable part of the body and most of us keep it more or less tight. Giving in and relaxing can even prove painful because it stretches the tight abdominal muscles. When you have (in your opinion) relaxed fully you can most likely give in a bit more. Take your time and work step by step.

How easy it is to relax your abdominal muscles will be affected by where you have your centre of gravity. Think about the first balancing exercise (see p. 57). It is easier to relax your abdomen with the weight more on the front of your feet and with free knees.

The area of bellybutton – pubic bone – pelvic floor – lower back is where all inhalation ought to have its origins. It begins with releasing these parts and allowing the air to stream in to the lungs. In this way this area is relaxed and ready to do its support work.

This deep and free relaxing stretches the muscles and the tissues involved. The recoil of these muscles and tissues is the start of the exhalation / support work.

PHONATION: ADDING VOICE

The crucial part of all voice work is the start. The start is not, as often thought, the beginning of the sound making. Voice work start some steps before, with the impulse to communicate. This impulse prepares, activates and adjusts the inhalation and changes the activity of the breathing muscles from only breathing for oxygen, into also giving an active support for the voice. If the inhalation is free and uninhibited, the body will also adjust the breath to what we want to say. The longer the thought or the more eager we are to be heard, the more air we will need and the more air the body will take in. This is something we naturally do when we speak in everyday life. In voice exercises it is easily forgotten. A mechanical exercise will never give the same result as one performed with the mind involved. We need to create an intention before voicing even in exercises. The intention for a sound is the starting point for the inhalation.

Training your voice is mostly about finding a more efficient way of using the body, you re-program your instrument. A balanced and relaxed body with a deep, uninhibited breathing is essential. The body will adjust its intake of air in relation to how much you have used in the phrase before, i.e. how much air there is left in the lungs. Never force or overexert your inhalation before the sound production starts. Doing this will create tensions and block the connection to the lower part of the abdomen. Leave the inhalation at peace and give your body the time needed to finish it.

Do you inhale through the nose or mouth? Do what is most comfortable for you. Inhaling through the nose moisturises and cleans the air a little; on the other hand the nostrils are narrow. When a lot of air is needed in a short time, the risk is that you suck the air in, instead of just letting it in. Inhaling through the nose easily creates tensions in the throat. I recommend breathing through the mouth – you get more air and a more released and deeper inhalation.

Remember that the air is the source of the sound. The air streams through the vocal folds and makes them vibrate. Have an image of the air as a firm and gentle pillar streaming up and out through your body. On top of this pillar of air the sound surfs or rides. Be generous with the air, never hold back, waste it and your breathing will be energized and enriched. Picture the sound streaming out of you as warm, ample, rich and soft.

> Yawn and pay attention to how the rear of the oral cavity widens and is lifted while the jaws open. Try to keep the tongue soft and forward in the mouth.

> Feel the beginning of a yawn, keep the sensation, and gently hum on an [m]. Release the [m] as a long and relaxed sigh. With the help of the sigh you will get a good amount of air flowing out of your body, air that carries the sound. Let the [m] gently slide down through your range.

> Do the same thing again and 'munch' softly on the [m]. Do you experience any vibrations in the forefront of the face and lips?

➢ Let the [m] gradually move into a vowel. 'mmmOo...'
[inhale] 'mmmAa...' [inhale] 'mmmIi...' [inhale] 'mmmEe...'

➢ Repeat and extend the sound. Direct the sound towards a
specific point at the other end of the room.

➢ Repeat but this time end the vowel on an [m]: 'mmOomm...'
Do this with both sliding sounds and sounds that stay on
one specific note. Don't let the final [m] ebb away. Keep the
energy, the airflow and the sound going until you decide to
finish the sound.

➢ Try again and now extend the phrase – combine the [m]
with different vowels into one long chain:
'mmmOommAammIimmEemm ≈...' Breathe before any
tensions start to sneak up on you.

  ● Keep the airstream going and work with legato.
    Always keep the image of the sound floating on top
    of the air pillar. The air carries the sound up in pitch
    and gently supports the sound from down under
    when it sinks in pitch.
  ● Remember that a sigh is an excellent start for the
    air stream.

➢ Try doing this in different pitches. Slide through your
comfortable range. Do not push for high or low notes –
they will come, but not by pushing. Pushing is contra
productive.

➢ Play with the sound by increasing and decreasing the
volume. Keep the airflow going and try to stay free
from tensions. Do not push for a big voice!

➢ Try the same thing with a gentle 'vavavav...' or
'momomom ...'

Make sure you have 'open knees' and let your body be in motion. Let the inhalation take care of itself and let it root deep down in the body. Remember: always work with a clear direction for the voice.

BALANCE AND STABILITY: LOWER ABDOMEN AND PELVIC MUSCLES

You need a functional, flexible muscle strength for voice work. This is in no way the same thing as a static gym build strength. This exercise builds on the exercise about balancing and centring your body while standing still (see p. 57). The principles of this exercise will also come back in the in-depth voice part.

This is an exercise that stimulates the activity in your legs and lower part of the torso. You need to work with activity and flexibility and avoid locking your joints or your breathing. You will grow in strength and energy as well as improve your poise and posture. The movements also help you find contact with the important muscles in your pelvic floor. Doing this exercise regularly not only stimulates that contact, it also builds strength in this area.

> ➢ Plant your feet firmly on the floor. The weight shall be on the entire foot but imagine the toes growing like roots forward into the floor.

> ➢ Make sure that you are open in ankles, knees and hips. Have the image that you are standing on the subway or a bus without holding on to anything. You need to parry the movements of the vehicle to keep your balance. You can only do that when the joints in your legs are open and ready to move.

Use the image of having a glass of water on your head and trying to keep it there, with the help of your ready-to-adjust open legs. The image helps you to keep your spine and head balanced.

➤ Explore the cooperation between gravity and your balance – how far can you move in any direction (without dropping the glass of water)?

➤ Tense your stomach – does this affect your balance?

➤ Release your stomach again – any difference?

➤ Try to keep the breathing low and free.

➤ Add a sound on an [f] or [s] – one movement and one sound. Let sound and movement have the same direction and energy.

➤ Add your voice, go from voiceless into voiced: [f] → [v] and [s] → [z] or do the earlier 'mmOom' exercise again.

*

➤ Skip the imaginary glass on your head and explore how much you can challenge your balance. Move freely around in soft movements.

- Change between both legs and one leg.
- How much can you bend, twist and turn?
- Where do you lose your balance?
- Can you slowly expand your limits for where you keep your balance?

➤ Keep your centre of gravity, with your knees free and your toes rooted.

Try to keep the airflow steady all the time. Play with sounds or a lip-trill. Many of the exercises in the book can also be done on a lip-trill. Work from voiceless to voiced trills. (Lip-trill is a common and brilliant exercise: see p. 113; many of the exercises herein can be done on a lip-trill).

> ➤ If you lose balance it is most likely because you locked some joint in your legs. Perhaps you cut off the airflow as well?

> ➤ Keep exploring and add some speaking and singing.

*

> ➤ Come back to standing firmly on both feet. Keep the thought that the floor might move a little and that you need to be prepared to parry. The feet are ready and so are ankles, knees and hips.

> ➤ There you have an excellent readiness in your body for voice work.

To think about the footpads and the legs as the motor for the voice is a good way to avoid tensions in the torso. To be firmly planted or rooted in the floor facilitates the airstream and supports the voice.

> ➤ An excellent tool to develop the exercise above with is a round balance board. Bravely climb the board, find your balance and repeat all the vocal tasks mentioned above.

> ➤ When you have found the balance and activity in your feet and legs return to the floor and try to maintain the activity from the balance board.

All helping tools including gestures or movements need to be abandoned in the end. We need to develop good body awareness without all the external crutches. We can't use them during a performance anyway.

VOCAL SUPPORT

All of us have already experienced support. When we cough or sneeze the support muscles are activated. When we cry or laugh until our stomach and sides ache, we use the support. When life is intensified – when we experience joy, pain or grief – we use the support like never before. Think of a crying infant. It is the centre of the infant's body that contracts in the outburst. Then comes a moment of relaxation and the body opens for the inhalation, until a new scream pours out. We have all had access to this optimal and spontaneous support at times in our life. Working with voice is very much about rediscovering this function and developing it further into the professional instrument we strive for.

Support is an extremely important part of all voice work. A well-functioning support is fundamental, be it speaking in public or on stage – from intimate love scenes to a big quarrel, from gentle speaking to full opera voice. In Beijing Opera it even has its own name: *Qi Chen Dantian*.

In all exercises for breathing and voice production, support is involved. The support is a delicate cooperation between different muscle groups. They create a solid, unbroken column of air, that sets the vocal folds into vibration. The support needs to be adapted to what is required by the voice in each situation. Factors that keep the air column stable and unbroken are: balanced back and neck, and a soft flexible muscle activity in the abdomen, pelvis and back. This is something you explored in the 'Balance and Stability' exercise above.

*

If you experience any tensions or feel uncomfortable in the larynx in the coming exercise it is most likely because you have tensed or stressed the respiratory system. Keep the image of the sound surf-riding on top of the air pillar, surfing up through and out of your body.

You should investigate the following exercise in lying, sitting and standing positions. Notice any differences. Keep in mind that the support is a smoother and more flexible work than we usually think. During the exercise, you must give the muscles the time needed to take and recover breath.

> Take an [f] and let it change into a [v] and notice what happens in the support area during the transition.
> Same thing with the [s] to [z].

> Feel how deep in the body you can experience an increased muscular activity, and how this affects the airflow.
> Also notice how soft the activity can be.

> Extend the sound until you feel any tensions sneaking up anywhere: in the stomach, diaphragm, chest, shoulders, neck and/or jaw. In that moment, you have disturbed the airflow and the support.

> Extend the sound again, but finish it just before the tensions arise. This time you have maintained the free support.

> Continue to gradually extend the sound further, but always finish before tensions arise.

> Remember to direct the airflow or sound toward a specific point in the room.

> Imagine that the sound is entering your body with the in-streaming air, that your body opens and expands to make room for the sound. Different sounds need different space. In a way you 'inhale' the sound.

> Imagine the release of the sound as an extension of the inhalation.

> ➤ Examine this further in speaking and think in the same way. 'Inhale' the line before you speak it – and keep the openness during the phrase. Try the same in singing.

Remember that support is a softer and more flexible work than most of us think. We *release* the air with help of the support – we do not push it out.

You should try to always use support, even in your everyday life. In this way, you do not have one way of using your voice in everyday life and a different one on stage. Moreover, it is a healthy habit that relieves the voice from unnecessary wear.

CAPACITY AND FLEXIBILITY IN YOUR BREATHING

It is important to train the capacity and flexibility of your breathing. We need to be able to adapt our breathing to the demands of the situation and the text. A great thought or a long phrase requires more air than a simple thought or a short phrase. Different sizes of rooms or theatres require different activity in your breathing.

A speaker or singer who is in full contact with what is communicated, and the reasons behind it, hardly ever runs out of breath. If the body and the breath are free and relaxed they work together with what is being said. It happens organically.

An important thing to keep in mind during all breathing and voice work is to never hold back your breath in an attempt to 'save' it. This only creates tensions. There is plenty of air in your lungs, waste it in every phrase and your breathing will be energized and become increasingly easy.

Examine how long you can extend an exhalation *without tensing up*. If it becomes difficult to release for the inhalation, then you probably have let the exhalation last too long and some tension has sneaked up on you. Bear in mind the exercises about support. Make sure you take the time needed to release belly button – pubic bone –

pelvic floor – lower back area for each inhalation. Inhale the sound that will follow and then let it surf out on top of the air.

> Feel that you are balanced, centred and relaxed. Feel the length and width of your spine.

> Try different exhalation lengths on [s], [f], [z], [v] or use a lip-trill.

> Direct the sound toward a fixed point at eye level in front of you.

> Try to gradually extend the exhalations, ten, fifteen, twenty seconds... It should still be easy to inhale! Let no tension sneak into your shoulders, neck or jaw.

> Try to count out loud, use an energized voice: 1 [inhale] 1≈2 [inhale] 1≈2≈3 [inhale] 1≈2≈3≈4 and continue to expand by one number at a time on one breath, as long as it feels comfortable. Do not forget to direct the numbers to a specific point in the room. Work with legato, it is 1≈2≈3 and not 1. 2. 3. with a stop between the numbers.

> Do the same with a piece of text, expand with one word at a time:

> > To [inhale]
> >
> > To be [inhale]
> >
> > To be or [inhale]
> >
> > To be or not [inhale]
> >
> > To be or not to [inhale]
> >
> > To be or not to be [inhale] ...

Here the example comes from *Hamlet* but you can try it with all kinds of texts.

> Investigate further by switching between long and short phrases:

$$1 \approx 2 \approx 3 \text{ [inhale]}$$

$$1 \text{ [inhale]}$$

$$1 \approx 2 \approx 3 \approx 4 \approx 5 \approx 6 \text{ [inhale]}$$

$$1 \approx 2 \text{ [inhale]}$$

...and so on.

Decide how long the next phrase shall be before you begin. This decision will affect your inhalation and preparation.

> Do the same with different kinds of texts. Switch between long and short phrases.

Never force or speed up your inhalation – let it evolve at a natural pace and breathe with your body's need for air. Pay attention to whether you shorten your inhalation or start to speak before the inhalation is fully done. When the outgoing phrase lengthens you will notice that your back becomes involved and participates in the inhalation. It expands.

> Repeat any of the exercises above but this time try to maintain the sensation of the open and expanded inhalation area during the phonation. Try to keep in contact with this area and stay open and wide, but without tension! More a feeling of that this area is floating out and up during the sound making. It is a feeling only, never mind what really happens.

The amount of air we inhale should match the thought and the emotion. I cannot stress enough how breathing and thinking go together. We have an impulse to say something so we inhale, then we exhale with sound. We speak or sing on the exhalation-air. Cicely Berry wrote in *The Actor and the Text*:

'Unless we recognize that the breath and the thought are one, no amount of breathing exercises will give purpose to the breath; will make it organic to what we are saying.'

'PLACING THE VOICE' – RESONANCE, DYNAMICS AND RANGE

'Placing the voice' is to be able to find a healthy resonance in the vocal tract (the cavities of the throat, mouth and nose). How we use and shape the vocal tract affects the overtones in our voice and helps us to 'place' the sound out in the room. We can't really place the voice anywhere such as in the head or chest but thoughts such as 'I open my skull' helps us to shape the vocal tract into an efficient sound box.

A good placement is important for anyone who uses their voice a lot. The placement, together with a feeling of 'lightness' of the voice, facilitates the function of the vocal folds and increases the vocal freedom in range and dynamics. Resonance, dynamics and range go hand in hand in voice work, but first comes the resonance, the placement. The placement is a premise to develop range and dynamics in a healthy way.

The basic conditions for an efficient placement is a good balance between energy and muscle activity together with a connected and free airflow. All the muscles surrounding the jaw, neck and throat, together with the muscles of the tongue, are involved. To develop a good body awareness in this area might be a bit tricky. Different images usually help more than anatomical descriptions.

*

Imagine your voice surfing on top of the air pillar somewhere at the level of your eyes, high above your vocal folds, throughout the coming exercises. Keep the sound focused and slim. Direct it out into the room. It shall be more like a laser beam than the widely scattered light from a light bulb.

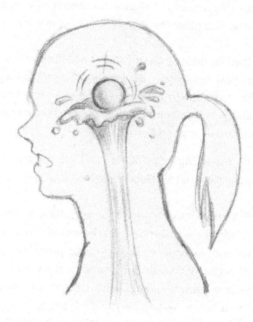

Another picture for the voice is a nozzle on a garden hose. You can turn the nozzle so that the water comes in a thin dense beam, or you can turn the nozzle so that the water spreads wide. It is the narrow dense beam that reaches the furthest. Same thing with the voice; a focused and slim voice reaches farther than an unfocused that spreads everywhere.

As always, work step by step. Do not primarily listen to your voice; experience the physical sensation of it in your body.

Finding placement

The following exercises will allow you to find and develop placement. Try each one and use those that help you the most. Remember that the proper amount of airflow is the source for a good placement.

Placement requires the same sort of precision that you would use when threading a needle. Imagine the sound as slim and precise as the thread, gently place the voice in the needle eye in front of you.

> ➤ Start by making an [m] sound which should be as slender as possible. Work with a focused sound, not a pushed one. Try to let the [m] vibrate – or buzz – somewhere within the area which encompasses your front teeth, hard palate and the tip of your nose.

We will be including a lot of [m] and [v] work in the upcoming exercises; use both in this slender and focused way.

> ➤ Start the sound on an [m] or a [v]. Have a clear point in the room where you will direct the sound. Think of a vowel behind the consonant wanting to 'jump' out. Focus on the direction of your [m] or [v] and let the vowel jump out of your mouth, the sound leaving the mouth and surfing out in the room. Make sure you don't reduce neither the airflow and the energy, nor the direction. It is a bit like throwing darts: the same focus and direction is needed yet the work is just as effortless. Repeat and change vowel. Avoid getting stuck in the nose so the vowel becomes nasal. This can easily happen after the [m].

> • Try to place the consonant somewhere in the front part of your hard palate. Let it create a buzz there. Aim to maintain that buzz-placing when you release the vowel.

➤ When the vowel jumps out behind [m] or [v], continue the phrase into 'va ≈ va ≈ vo ≈ vo ≈ vi ≈ vi'. Use whatever vowel you prefer. Try to imagine skimming stones. The stone needs a starting energy, the snatch from your wrist, and then it bounces on the surface of the water. Touching the surface of the water gives it a little bit of new energy to go on to the next bounce. Think of the consonant as that bounce, and the vowel as the flight over the surface. The bounce is easier to find on the [v] than on the [m]. As always, work on a continuous air-flow, with legato.

➤ Do it again and sustain the vowel, make sure it reaches the point you are directing the sound to. Imagine that it leaves your mouth and flies in an arch to that point: 'vaaa ≈ vooo ≈'. Make sure that you keep the energy going.

➤ Try to keep this placing, the buzz in the hard palate, and do all this again both in your speaking voice and your singing voice. Work through your entire comfortable range, in both modal and falsetto voice.

*

➤ Another way to discover placement is to gently pinch your nose bone. Make a 'hiii' sound and try to place the vowel so that the sound makes the bone of the nose buzz. Keep the sound going and let go of your nose. What happened to the sound?

● Keep the pinching and slide through your range. You will notice that the buzz in your nose disappears now and then. Try to direct the sound so you keep the buzz going, regardless of pitch. Try with different vowels.
● Again, let go of your nose and strive to keep the buzz.

- If the sound gets stuck in your nose, i.e. becomes too nasal, you have lowered the soft palate too much. Open your mouth a little bit more until the nasality disappears. Let the sound stream up under your hard palate on its way out of your mouth.
- You can also try to close the opening to the nose a bit by lifting the soft palate. For most of us the physical sensation is the opposite: it feels as if you lower the soft palate when you lift it and vice versa.

A free voice with an efficient resonance and a precise articulation, rather than the volume of the voice, is what makes the voice reach out into an auditorium.

Lightness

The voice needs not only to be slender and placed forward, it also needs 'lightness' all through the range. The feeling of lightness is a way to avoid digging down into your throat, it releases the vocal folds from wear and makes the vocal production more efficient. Lightness can easily be misunderstood as a high pitched or breathy voice, a voice without support. It is no such thing. On the contrary, lightness in the voice goes also for a deep basso. It is about the placement and function, the sound quality, not the pitch.

Sometimes different images or 'feelings' might help more than exact anatomic descriptions. Hopefully some of the following might help you to develop the placement and lightness further. Imagine the voice floating inside your head, somewhere in the height of your eyes. Keep the forward placement from the earlier exercises and bring that into the following ones.

➤ Use an 'ahAAaaaaa' sound and slide comfortably through your range. Imagine the sound as sailing light and high up under the roof of your mouth. Let the 'ahaaaa' sail right under your hard palate and out. Keep the lightness wherever you are in your range. Here are some images to help you find lightness and placement:

● the 'ahAA' when you finally understood something: 'ahAAaa, I got it!'
● the feeling of a nice surprise: 'The flowers are for me!?' kind of surprise. Where in your face do you feel the activity? Can you place an 'ahAA' there?
● the physical sensation when you smell something nice or when you try to identify a smell. Place the 'ahAA' there;
● the first sensation that a sneeze is imminent! Can you place the sound there?

*

Dynamics and range of voice are important to any speaker and most certainly so for an actor or singer. It is essential to be able to move smoothly between strong and soft voice, between different pitches, between speaking and singing; both in gradual and abrupt transitions.

A good placing helps you both with range and dynamics since it relieves the vocal folds. You need to maintain a lightness of the sound even in high energy voice. Try all of the following exercises both in speaking and singing. Don't forget the falsetto and keep all that you experienced during the previous exercises with you as well.

Dynamics

The risk when you increase the volume and power of your speech is that the voice goes up in pitch and you start to tense. The risk when lowering the volume is a loss of energy; the support might disappear and you can lose the direction in your speech.

It is particularly important in this exercise to maintain the release in the jaw, neck and shoulders as well as maintaining a stable airflow.

Keep in mind that the stronger the tone, the deeper you must breathe and the neck and the throat must be kept even more free and open. Keep your feet firmly rooted in the floor. Remember the placing from the previous exercise. Work in this placing with a slim and focused voice. It is a forward direction of the sound. Pay extra attention to this in diminuendo. It is the sound that weakens – not the energy. Sometimes the energy actually needs to increase when the volume goes down. It is more a feeling of holding the sound back rather than the airflow.

In the next exercise keep the image of the sound surfing on top of the air pillar all through the work and don't forget the clear direction. Remember the support exercise. If needed, sit behind your seat bones and rise slowly up on them during the phrase (see p. 88). As soon as you feel that you force or tense up, breathe and restart.

> ➢ Start off by taking a soft note on [m]. You should feel that the breath is anchored deep in the body. Open to a vowel and let the note gradually grow in intensity (crescendo). Make sure you keep the same pitch all the way.

> ➢ Take a new note on [m] and release it into a vowel. Gradually reduce the intensity (diminuendo) without losing the energy or pitch. Still, think as if you are slowly rising up on your seat bones during the diminuendo.

> ➢ This time make a crescendo and then make a diminuendo to an even weaker tone than the one you started on. Make the crescendo and diminuendo on one breath and on the same pitch. Notice if you tense somewhere. If you do: stop, relax and restart.

Crescendo and diminuendo on one breath and the same pitch is a classic voice exercise called *Messa di Voce* – an excellent exercise to gain control over the airflow and the vocal production.

> ➤ Examine all this in different pitches and sounds. Which are the most comfortable for you?

Remember the laser beam or the needle eye. Keep the focus, precision and the forward direction of the voice both in crescendo and in diminuendo. Keep the 'buzz' feeling in the hard palate all through the phrase. Avoid letting the voice spread and become 'big' in crescendo; increase the intensity, not the volume. In diminuendo, you need to avoid losing energy and focus. You will most likely need to increase your energy, rather than reduce it.

> ➤ Try speaking a line or singing a phrase, firstly as an ongoing crescendo, then as a diminuendo and lastly as a *Messa di Voce*.

Range

It is important to be aware of and have access to the full range of your voice. In everyday life, most of us use a narrow range. As a professional speaker you need to have a wide range and to be able to speak in many different pitches. This provides a greater freedom in the ability to modulate the speech. To have a wide and comfortable range is even more important to a singer. The risk when going up in pitch is to tense the neck, jaw and tongue and when you go down in pitch to 'push' the note down and tense the larynx. Be aware of this and try to keep the relief in the neck and jaw through the exercises.

> ➤ Pay attention to where you have your breathing.
> Create space and prepare for the sound already during your inhalation.

> ➤ Make a soft 'ho' sound in the upper range of your speaking
>   (modal) voice, slide comfortably down on the vowel
>   through your range and finish it on [m] in your deepest,
>   but still comfortable, range. Try this with different vowels.
>   Take help of the [h] to make the airflow ample and soft
>   already from the start. 'hOom' through your comfortable
>   range. Make sure you do not push down the sound.

Imagine that with the inhalation you create a space for the sound high up in your skull. At the same time as the sound slides down to your lowest range, imagine that you open and expand your skull. In a way, the deeper the note the higher the placement of it. This is to avoid digging and pushing down the sound. Keep a lightness in the voice all the way down to your lowest range.

Make sure that the air carries the sound all the way up, out and forward into a specific point in the room. Our deepest sounds are always weaker than the higher ones. Don't try to push out more volume. Use the resonance instead to focus the sound, and in this way make it more audible. It is healthier and more efficient. It will be a smaller sound in your head but a bigger sound out in the room. You have placed the sound at the listener instead of enjoying the big boom in your own skull.

> ➤ Now change the direction of the sound and pick the 'ho'
>   sound from a specific point in the room. Imagine that you
>   drag or inhale it through your mouth and let it come out
>   through an imagined opening in the back of your head.
>   Let the sound pass over your head and back to the point
>   you picked it from. The sound travels in an ellipse.

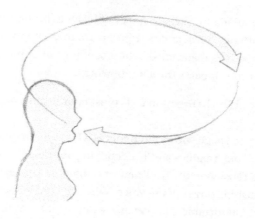

This way of 'picking up' the sound might help you find the placing in the skull. Try both directions in the upcoming exercises. Picking up the sound from, or directing it to, a specific point in the room.

> Slide from your deepest comfortable sound to your highest comfortable sound in your speaking range. Start on an [m]. Open for a vowel and make a crescendo 'mmmaaaAAA'. Keep the slim, focused sound and the feeling of lightness all through the exercise.

> Examine the same thing on different vowels.

> If you feel that the air is running out or that you tense, then relax, breathe and continue. Remember that the air is the driving force.

> Try the exercises in different positions: standing, sitting and lying.

This image might help you: between the top of your head and the pelvic floor is an open elevator shaft that the elevator – i.e. the sound – slides through. Regardless of where the elevator is, the shaft must remain open.

> ➤ Count aloud, or read a piece of text, all through your range. Both top-down and bottom-up. Do this with the different directions mentioned before, sending out or picking up. Let the air carry the sounds/words.

> ● Which direction feels most comfortable for you?

> ➤ Try to speak with a pitch that is a bit high up in your range and one that lies a little deeper in your range. Remember: no tension in the neck, jaw or tongue, or 'squeezing' or 'pushing down' of the voice. When the pitch is a little uncomfortable it is even more important that the air carries the sound and that you keep the lightness.

With a good function of the voice you should be able to speak in both a high-pitched and a low-pitched voice, somewhere above or under what is most comfortable for you. Furthermore, you should be able to do so in an effortless but energetic way. This is possible when breathing, support and placing of the voice all work well together.

When you expand your range it is easy to get a crack, a break in your voice, an abrupt change of vocal quality. Never mind that. It is only the vocal folds changing oscillation pattern. This is natural and something you can work on. If you have a cold or are tired, that crack might be pronounced.

If you want to avoid the crack, be aware that it is more pronounced with forced work. Try to work smoother, with greater airflow and slowly 'sneak' up through the cracking area. Maintain the open space in your skull, let the sound surf all the way up under your skull bone. You can try both pinch-the-nose and directing the sound up-in-the-skull. See what helps you the most, it might vary in different pitches. Nothing is a 'once and for all' in voice work.

TRILLING WITH YOUR LIPS

This is an excellent exercise, one of my absolute favourites. It can be a little tricky to get hold of, but it is worth spending the time mastering it. When you find the way to do it, it will always be there with you. It is easy, efficient and needs no special space or tools. I do it with beginners as well as with professional opera singers.

The exercise helps you work with the support and the airflow. It trains the capability for sustained phrases. Being able to spin a sound or note without holding back the airflow is an important skill for a singer or actor. Voice requires significantly more air than most of us think. Waste the air and your breathing capacity will be improved and energized. You will also notice that you have much more air than you imagined.

The lip-trill creates a slight resistance for the air that stimulates the activity of your supporting muscles. The resistance also relieves the larynx and the vocal folds. Furthermore, the fast changes in air pressure above the vocal folds (supraglottal), coming from the opening and closing of the lips, spread down to the vocal folds and 'massage' them. It is an excellent way both to warm up your voice and to make the folds relax after intensive work.

Pout *softly* with the lips and blow the air through them so that the (voiceless) lip-trilling starts. It needs a firmer air-flow than you might expect. A firm, ample and steady air-flow, not a hard or pushed one.

> ➤ Try to find the least amount of air that makes the lip-trill work.

> ➤ Try to keep the trilling steady all through the airstream. Don't use harder airstream or bigger amount of air than necessary.

> ➤ When this goes smoothly, add voice: trill voicing, on a note.

> ➤ Trill through your comfortable range.

> ➤ Extend the range a bit, both up and down.

> ➤ Add a *Messa di Voce* all through your range, one pitch at a time.

Make sure the trilling works all the way. If not, try to find the reason for why it did not work. Most likely you lost the stability in the airflow.

Trilling can tickle a lot in your face and lips. Endure this. It's just the upper lip that is being freed from tensions.

> ➤ When you are confident with the lip trilling, 'sing' a song trilling. Take time to really trill, with help of the airstream, through the song.

>> ● You will notice that if the trill gets into trouble it is likely to be where you have difficulties when you sing the song. Take your time to really trill through the tricky passage. Usually it is a lack of airflow that is the problem.

> ➤ Trilling is also a good way to work with extended phrase length. As always, work slowly and pay attention so that no tension sneaks up on you.

> ➤ Trilling is a superb way to work with your songs. Lip-trill your song a couple of times and then go back to sing it. Maintain the energy built up from the trilling into the singing and see what difference it makes.

The trilling is a good image of how the vocal folds function. The lips are softly closed, the air pressure builds up behind them and blows them apart. The air streams out, the pressure goes down and the lips close again. The air pressure builds up again and blows the lips apart. This is a cycle similar in function to the opening/closing phase of the vocal folds.

*

This trilling is a good exercise to bring into the in-depth section. Most exercises there benefit from some skilful lip trilling. You can use the lip-trill in most of the exercises in this book. However, if it turns out to be absolutely impossible to make a lip-trill you can always replace it with a voiceless or voiced 'tip of the tongue' – trill [r] or the usual [f/v] and [s/z]. They all help with resistance of the airflow.

ARTICULATION

We speak to express a need or a thought with help of words. We can express the importance of the words through the articulation; by giving them their proper weight and clarity. Then we have a meaningful articulation. Microphones and loudspeakers only support the volume; they will not make the words clearer or more urgent.

*

When the sound reaches the mouth, we use the tongue, lips, teeth, jaw and soft palate to split up and shape it to meaning-bearing units: speech sounds, syllables and words. The most important articulator is the tongue. To function in an optimal way the tongue needs a relaxed and flexible jaw, something that gives space for its movements in the oral cavity.

The vowels are the free voiced sounds where the air passes out without hindrance. The consonants are the sounds, voiced or voiceless, where the airflow is hampered in varying degrees by the articulators.

The articulation, together with the placement of the voice, is what helps us to be heard. A precise and energetic articulation is of more importance than volume. When faced with tricky acoustics or really big rooms the articulation is of much more help than trying to make the voice loud or big. Someone with impaired hearing will find a crisp articulation more helpful than a loud voice.

It is absolutely possible to have a good and precise articulation in singing. Energetic or precise consonants are in no way a contradiction to a maintained legato. In fact it's the opposite. A good articulation facilitates a good support and airflow. You can even use the consonants as a springboard to reach tricky pitches. Sing on the air through the consonants. Furthermore, the articulation relieves and supports the vocal folds both in speaking and singing.

Exercising the articulation can be done easily.

> Let the jaw and tongue hang relaxed, the tongue resting softly against the lower teeth. The tongue is the floor of the oral cavity and the hard palate is the ceiling. Try to picture the oral cavity's space.

> Let the tip of the tongue explore the palate from front to back and side to side. Can you feel where the hard palate ends and the soft palate begins? Can you feel that the palate is arch-shaped? The arch-shape helps to amplify the sound waves in the outflowing sound.

> Read a text aloud. Take your time to discover the activity of your articulators. Really 'taste' the text and the different speech-sounds in it.

- Pay attention to when the tip of the tongue, the middle or the rear part is active.
- What parts of the mouth does the tongue touch: teeth, soft or hard palate, lips?
- Notice the tongue's movements and transitions between different positions while you speak.

- Pay attention to the mobility of the joint of the jaw.
- Notice how the opening of your mouth changes size and shape.
- How is the activity of the lips?
- Is the soft palate activated now and then?
- Does the language you speak have any sounds that are made in the lower vocal tract?
- Imagine that the articulators softly mould the airflow into words.
- Breathe as soon as you need.

The following exercise is a workout exercise for the articulators, where you over-exaggerate the articulation. Keep the work free from tensions and make sure that the airflow is involved. Keep the sounds correct, do not end up in some 'funny' way of speaking. Work slowly and pay attention to the different articulators' transitions from one place to the next. Use a short text and repeat until you feel that you have gained a crispy, clear and precise articulation.

➤ Read aloud and overdo the articulation.

- First the consonants. Give them some more energy than usual: 'spit' them out. Make them really distinct.
- Then the vowels. Give them some extra time and make them clear and precise.
- Thereafter mould each speech sound and keep the legato. Don't end up in staccato – work softly and still with high precision and energy.

Strive for continuous transitions between the speech sounds. Give the speech sounds the time needed and the exact shape – regardless of your language or accent. Make sure that your jaw and tongue work effortlessly and with energy. Try to keep the content of the text in mind.

> ➢ Speak the text again. This time work with the text and articulation in a relaxed way and see if the previous exercise led to a higher precision.

Remember that it is not about being able to shoot out syllables but having a high intelligibility. It is important that you hold the content of the text in mind during the exercise, so you don´t end up in mechanical articulation.

> ➢ Do all of these exercises with your song lyrics as well. Speak the lyrics in the over-articulated way a couple of times and then sing them.

*

An exact and involved articulation will feel peculiar in the beginning, especially when you strive to master it. When the muscles have grown used to the work, and you have become accustomed to speaking in this more energetic way, it will feel totally natural and organic. Once it feels natural for you it will appear natural for the listener as well. Remember that people only complain when they cannot hear or understand what was said; be it in everyday life or from stage or screen. No one complains because they heard too well!

When we are involved in what we are talking or singing about, when it is imperative that we are listened to and understood, when we want to persuade; then we all articulate with higher precision and energy. On the other hand, slack articulation sends the signal that we are not so involved in what we are saying, a 'this is not really important' signal to the listener. Slack articulation is slack thinking. We can afford neither if we want to be listened to.

In-depth Voice Work

In this section we develop the skills and awareness you have already worked with into a professional singing or speaking voice. We will address the same issues: a balanced body and breathing, a free neck and jaw and an uninhibited mind. We work with even higher energy and activity in the body and a clear focus on what we aim for with the professional voice. In this section the exercises are more demanding and it's important that you spend a proper amount of time on each of them. Exploring and learning takes time: our brain understands faster than our body does.

When we speak our own words and thoughts we automatically adjust our breathing and vocal range to the purpose of our speech. When we express someone else's words we need to explore the thinking behind them. This knowledge helps us to prepare for the vocal demands that will follow. As an actor or singer you need to be aware of the vocal challenge in the text or song before you throw yourself at it. Knowing the physical demands of the phrase ahead is crucial. For example, how long is the phrase or how wide is the song's range? It is like choreography; you need to be familiar with each step before you start to dance.

What you know intellectually or emotionally about the text or song has to be transformed into a physical knowledge. Your body needs to know which path to take that allows you to sing or speak with confidence. It is during practise and rehearsal we discover what to anticipate; it is there we pave the road to avoid disturbing surprises.

Your preparation for a phrase begins with the inhalation. You prepare and embrace the technical challenges ahead of you together with the thoughts and the emotions; you open up both your body and mind for what will come. To open up your body and mind is to be able to stand 'naked' in front of people, free from muscle tensions as well as tensions or obstructions in your mind. This will help you, not only technically, but also to access your impulses. The aim is to remain open.

EXTENDED BREATHING WHILE ON YOUR BACK

The following exercise encourages you to discover the different muscles involved in the deep and big breathing needed for a heightened voice. Throughout this exercise avoid interfering with your inhalation: just be aware of it.

> ➤ Rest on your back and scan through your body. If you need to release your neck from strain, place a thin book (or something similar) under your head.

> ➤ Wriggle your feet, knees, hips, spine, breastbone, shoulder blades and finally let your head gently roll from side to side. Don't forget to release your jaw.

>> ● Can you feel if there are any remaining tensions or stresses? Take your time to release these before you move on to the next part of your body.
>> ● What do you find most comfortable: legs straight or bent?

> ➤ Pay attention to your relaxed breathing.

>> ● Which parts of your body move when the air streams in?
>> ● Which parts move when the air streams out again?
>> ● Do you stop, inhibit or increase the speed of your breathing at any moment?
>> ● Do you breathe through your mouth or nose?

➤ Gently prolong your exhalation on an [f] sound but ensure it is comfortable.

- During the subsequent inhalation how are the movements in your body affected?
- How does this inhalation then affect the muscular activity in the following [f] exhalation?

➤ Continue gently prolonging the exhalation on pulses of [f] sound.

- Add one [f] for each new exhalation: make sure the [f] sounds are connected in each phrase. Work with legato.
- Continue to add a new [f]-pulse for each new breath but stop before you experience any tension or any difficulty in relaxing for the inhalation.

> ff [inhale]
>
> ff ≈ ff [inhale]
>
> ff ≈ ff ≈ ff [inhale]
>
> ff ≈ ff ≈ ff ≈ ff [inhale]
>
> ff ≈...

➤ When you have reached your maximum amount of [f]s, without becoming tense, reduce one [f] for each breath until you have reached a single [f] in the exhalation.

- How does your body and breathing feel when you reduce the length of the phrase compared with when you expanded it?

➤ Roll over on to your side and then stand up slowly (you might be a bit dizzy after all that breathing).

➤ Repeat the exercise, this time while standing.

- What happened to your muscle activity this time?
- Did you notice anything different and if so, what?

The focus of this exercise is to pay attention to how the exhalation and inhalation affect each other.

- Which muscles are involved: abdomen, chest, sides, back... any others?
- What happens when the length of the phrase increases?
- What happens when the length of the phrase decreases?
- Is there any point at which you have forced the breathing? Quickened it? Shortened it? If yes, when has this occurred in the breathing process and whereabouts in your body?

If you are curious, go back and look at the anatomy part about the respiratory muscles after you have finished the exercise. There is a risk that you interfere with the 'organic' function of your body if you do this before, something that can be counterproductive and diminish the value of the exercise.

THE BEETLE EXERCISE

Here comes The Beetle, so named by some of my students. It is a very efficient exercise but it takes a bit of time to get the hang of. In the beginning, you need to spend at least three to four minutes on each step. To do a full Beetle (once you're familiar with it) takes around twenty minutes, depending on how you do it – but then both your body and voice should be fully warmed up and ready for work.

The Beetle challenges your coordination, flexibility and strength and improves each efficiently. It builds up a smooth flexible strength in the muscles of the torso, muscles that are central for the support. It 'oils' your joints, releases your muscles from tension and increases your body awareness. I cannot stress enough the importance of being mentally present in this exercise. Your mind needs to be with your body all the time.

Before you begin you'll need to find enough space so that you can freely move around on the floor. Avoid carpets that will hamper your movements and steer clear of furniture which you might accidently smack into.

Let's start. What you need to do is to lie on the floor working with all four limbs simultaneously but independently (just like a beetle stuck on its back). Keeping the movements going you slowly bring yourself up so that you are standing. Don't be alarmed by the snapping, cracking and crunching that you might hear. Keep oiling your joints with the movements. Work rather slowly, but not in slow-motion, and with a light resistance, almost as if you are moving through water.

Take your time to explore your body and challenge your coordination and flexibility. As always adjust to your current condition. And don't forget to read the full exercise before you start.

STEP ONE: A LIMB AT A TIME

Right arm

➤ Begin by lying on your back on the floor. Take your time to relax.

- Pay attention to your breathing – is it free or inhibited? Throughout the first part of this exercise leave your breathing be, just make sure you don't block it.

➤ Gently move the fingers on your right hand.

- Move all the finger joints. Can you notice how many joints your fingers have? The rest of your body should be heavily relaxed.
- Let your breathing stay free and undisturbed.

➤ Let the movement spread and involve your hand.

➤ Spread the movement to your wrist.

  ● In how many ways can your wrist joint move?

➤ Involve your elbow.

  ● Now you have engaged the fingers, hand, wrist and elbow in the movement. The rest of the body should be relaxed.

➤ The movement now spreads to the shoulder joint and then the shoulder blade.

  ● Now all five fingers move independently, as do the hand, wrist, elbow, shoulder and shoulder blade.
  ● The rest of the body remains relaxed and the breathing should be uninhibited.
  ● Pay attention to the movements you are making but don't get stuck on the same one all the time. Change direction every now and then. Discover what your body actually can do.

➤ Let your arm come to rest.

  ● Notice the difference between the right and left arm.

This then is the basis of the Beetle. Repeat the exercise with all four limbs, one by one. At a later stage in the Beetle the limb movements will be combined in different ways.

Now work diagonally, so on to the **left leg**.

➤ Gently move the toes on your left foot.

- Can you move all your toes independently?

➤ Spread the movement to your foot and ankle. The rest of your body should be relaxed.

➤ Involve your knee and keep the toes and ankle moving.

- What can you do with your knee if the hip is still passively relaxed (notice how little you can do)?

➤ Involve your hip. Discover how that joint works.

- Now move your left leg all the way from toes, foot, ankle, knee to hip.
- Try to incorporate as many different movements as you can imagine.

➤ Slowly let your leg come to rest.

- Compare the left with the right leg.

Continue with the **right leg**.

➤ Gently move the toes of your right foot.

- Can you move all five independently?

➤ Spread the movement to your foot and ankle. The rest of the body should be relaxed.

➤ Involve your knee and ensure that your toes, foot and ankle keep moving.

- What can your knee do if the hip is still relaxed (still not very much)?

➤ Involve your hip. Discover how that joint works.

- Compare this hip with how the left hip was.
- Now move your right leg all the way from toes, foot, ankle, knee to hip.
- Try to use as many different movements as you can imagine.

➤ Compare working with your right leg to working with the left leg.

➤ Slowly let your leg come to rest.

- Compare your right leg with your left in rest.

And now the **left arm**.

> ➤ Gently move the finger joints of your left hand.
>
>> ● The rest of your body should be heavily relaxed and your breathing is free.
>
> ➤ Let the movement spread and involve the hand.
>
> ➤ Spread the movement to the wrist.
>
>> ● In how many ways can your wrist joint move?
>
> ➤ Involve the elbow.
>
>> ● Now engage your fingers, hand, wrist and elbow in the movements all the while ensuring that the rest of your body is relaxed. Compare this side to how the right side was.
>
> ➤ The movement spreads to the joint of the shoulder and then the shoulder blade.
>
>> ● Now all five fingers are moving independently, so are the hand, wrist, elbow, shoulder and shoulder blade.
>> ● You should keep the rest of your body relaxed and your breathing should be uninhibited.
>> ● Pay attention to which movements you are using – don't get stuck on the same one all the time. Change direction now and then. Discover what your body is capable of.
>
> ➤ Does your left arm feel similar to the right?
>
> ➤ Now let the arm come to rest.
>
>> ● Notice any differences between the right and left arm.

STEP TWO: COMBINING YOUR LIMBS

(This is where you can start once you have mastered **Step One**.)

Remember that the parts of your body that has yet to be activated should be relaxed and your breathing should remain free.

From one limb to two diagonally, to three and finally all four limbs

➤ Begin with your right hand's fingers.

- Let the movement slowly spread joint by joint, just like in Step One. Fingers, hand, wrist, elbow, shoulder joint and shoulder blade.
- When you have reached the right shoulder blade it is time to start engaging the 'diagonal' limb, the left leg.

➤ Now start moving the toes on your left foot; keep the movement of the right arm going.

- Joint by joint you involve the left leg: toes, foot, ankle, knee and hip.
- Keep your right arm moving.
- Keep the breathing free.

➤ From the fingertips of your right hand to the toes of your left foot you will now be activated diagonally through the torso.

➤ Activate the toes of the right foot, the rest of the leg stays relaxed and the breathing is free.

- Involve, one at a time, the foot, ankle, knee and finally the hip.
- Now you are moving your right arm and both your legs.

➤ Start moving your left fingers and slowly spread the movement, joint by joint, to the shoulder blade.

- You are by now moving all four limbs at the same time but independently. Try to feel the connection from the fingertips to the toes.
- Do you have contact with all your body or is any part forgotten or out of touch?
- Is your breathing still inhibited?

As soon as you feel comfortable with the Beetle, you can vary the starting point: left or right side, fingers or toes. In this way you will continue to challenge and develop your body awareness and coordination.

STEP THREE: ENGAGE ALL YOUR BODY

> Spread the movements from your limbs into your torso and up to your neck. Contract, stretch out, turn and twist all your body. Make sure you get all four sides of your torso opened up and stretched. Keep all the joints in your body moving.

This is a bit of work for the muscles in your torso, a flexible work – it is not gym. Remember 'Stretch exercise for the breathing' (see p. 69). Try to open up your torso just as much as in that exercise.

Take your time in the following: spend at least some minutes on each step.

> Prolong your exhalation a bit on [s] or [f]. Leave your inhalation in peace.

> Let the exhalation be on a [z], [v] or [m]. Keep turning and twisting and moving. Open up your chest and your back.

> Let the exhalation be on a lip trill. Start voiceless and go into a voiced trill.

➢ Keep moving and slowly come up in standing. Keep the sounds going.

➢ When up in standing, plant your feet firmly on the ground, massage or 'glue' the palm of your feet against the floor.

➢ Keep all your body moving – soft and gentle movements.

  ● An image can be seaweed, the roots are deep down in the seabed and the branches move freely with the water.

Keep the breathing active and free. Let the inhalation take place wherever it likes to in the body. Place the outgoing sound at a specific spot in the room.

➢ Use a voiced lip trill and play with the sound:

  ● Crescendo – diminuendo (*Messa di Voce*)
  ● Glissandi through your comfortable range
  ● Do all this in both your modal voice and your falsetto

Build up your vocal energy by involving all your body. Get the power from your roots – your feet on the floor. Let the direction of your body and voice cooperate. Direct the sound to the same spot your body is moving towards.

➢ Keep the work going and speak or sing during the activity.

  ● Whenever you need to inhale – do so, even in the middle of a phrase.

STEP FOUR: KEEP THE INNER ENERGY

➤ With this activated and uninhibited body – with high energy in your body, breathing and voice – slow down your movements so that your body becomes still but keep the inner energy and activity going.

➤ Strive to keep the energy in the voice going even when your body isn't moving.

➤ Find a way to keep the activity and flexibility acquired during the exercise within your still body.

Here we have reached the end of a full Beetle. By now you are hopefully warmed up: flexible, free and energized in both body and voice.

FINDING THE SUPPORT WITH THE IMAGE OF AN INTERNAL RUBBER BAND

In my experience most of us use too little energy in voice making. Voice work takes energy and activity both in inhaling and in sound making. When the task demands high energy and activity it is even more important to work free of tensions.

*

For a more stable support, something that is needed in singing and speaking from a stage, we need to develop a firmer muscular control of the air-flow. The support area is the lower abdomen and the back. The abdomen goes down/out and the back goes out/up, in a firm yet soft movement. The body expands and the air streams in.

A way to find a connection between the lower abdomen and the back is to imagine a rubber band attached to the pubic bone and the inside of your back (see over).

Imagine that this rubber band, the kind that is used in physiotherapy, is attached to three points: the pubic bone and each side of your middle back. When you relax for an inhalation the lower part of your stomach goes down/out. The inhalation spreads like a wave to the sides of your back which also expands a little. The inhalation expands your body and softly stretches the internal rubber band. You continue to stretch and expand the rubber band throughout the phrase.

By keeping the expansion from the inhalation in the following sound-making/exhalation you keep the torso open, which will give you a better access to the air you have. This openness is part of the firm and flexible support. The movement is adaptable and depends upon what you like to do with your voice; the firmness of the stretching of the rubber band can be stronger or softer. However, the rubber band mustn't slacken or tense up – it must always stay flexible.

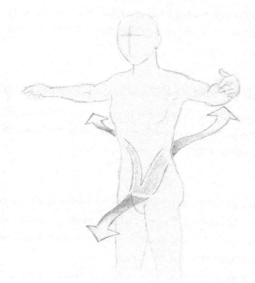

Let the inhalation be followed by the sound making in one connected movement. Envisage it like this: you inhale the phrase and thereafter release it. The air streams in and out, like a wave rolling up on to a beach and then back out to sea, with no stop or blocking. Imagine the expansion from the inhalation continuing to float out and upwards while you make the sound.

Be aware of the placement when trying out this exercise.

➤ Try first on a lip-trill to make a soft *Messa di Voce* and feel how the rubber band stretches for the crescendo and softly gives in a bit for the diminuendo.

➤ Once you are more familiar with the image, try singing a song on a lip-trill, paying attention to how the 'rubber-band' area is activated during the song.

➤ Thereafter skip the lip-trill and sing with the lyrics.

> ➤ Finally speak with a high energy voice. The activity should be more or less the same regardless of how you use your voice.

PLACING OF THE VOICE: HOW TO INCREASE RESONANCE AND RANGE

An optimum placing of the voice is important for the freedom of the vocal folds. This placing is not a fixed point, it is flexible and changes with pitch, vowel and intended sound quality.

*

As always, pay attention to how you stand and how ready your body is for energized breathing. Keep your knees free and open. Keep in mind the breath-stretching exercise and the 'extended breathing' you did on your back (see pp. 69 & 120).

It is really important that you stay free from tension. Pay close attention to any tension that sneaks into your shoulders. They can affect the clavicula and breastbone and spread to the muscles around the larynx. Tension in your shoulders can also spread to your neck. Neck, jaw and tongue affect each other and hence the freedom of the larynx and the vocal folds.

Exploring vibrations

We start with exploring where in the body there can be vibrations. These are physical sensations of the sound waves which spread in all directions – upwards and downwards – from the vocal folds. If you keep free from tension the oscillating air can set your bones and harder tissues in vibrations. These vibrations can be carried throughout the body. They arise with help of the airflow and your released body – you cannot force them.

This exercise will help you locate where the vibrations can occur.

> Hum on an [m] and play around in a range that's comfortable to you. Check with your hands to see if there are any vibrations in your body and notice how they feel. Take your time to explore the crown, the back of the head, your forehead, cheekbones, jaw, neck, sternum, ribs, back, leg.

> What happens with the vibrations if you open for a vowel?

> Are there any changes if you make the sounds stronger or weaker?

Do you experience vibrations in more than one place at the same time?

Repeat the exercise above with this next image in mind and see if anything changes.

Your upper body is an empty vessel from the pelvic floor to the top of your skull, supported only by your legs and feet. Picture how your every breath expands and fills all your upper body from bottom to top with air. Imagine that this openness remains when you exhale, like your upper body soars or floats outwards. Imagine that your voice is free to move around inside this empty space, regardless of what note you pick. Bear in mind that you cannot force the vibrations. They must occur by themselves.

Vibrations can occur more or less anywhere in the body and are usually a sign of a free body and voice. A free body facilitates the work with placement. However, the vibrations mustn't be confused with placement. The perception or sensation of vibrations are highly individual. Someone might feel a buzz in their cheekbones whereas somebody else senses it in their skull or chest bone and another person might not feel any vibrations at all.

Placement

The Italian singing teacher Giovanni Battista Lamperti fils (1839–1910) said 'Using low resonance alone has ruined every voice that tried it.'[1] I am inclined to agree with him. To be able to project the voice out into a bigger space or to be heard in a noisy environment you need to further enhance the voice with resonance in the face and head. Whatever pitch you are in, an optimal placing is a resonance above the vocal folds.

The next step is to try to find an efficient voice placement. Keep the awareness and the feeling of an open and vibrating body into the coming exercise.

*

Let's move on to placement and resonance in the head. We use the [m] which is a nasal sound that is placed forward in the mouth and the cavity of the nose. This is a good starting point to find placement.

> ➢ Hum on an [m]: feel that it is so far in the front of your mouth that it tickles the lips.

> ➢ Let the [m] transfer into [e] and feel the tickling of your lips continue into the vowel. Make sure that the focus of your energy and voice is very forward in your mouth. Don't let the nasal [m] mislead you into making the vowel nasal as well.

> ➢ Now start again with [m] and let it transfer into all the other vowels one at a time (don't get nasal).

> ➢ Now try beginning directly on a vowel instead. Aim for the energy to be just as forward as on [m]. Do it a couple of times, using different pitches. Change the vowel you use every now and then.

> ➢ Perform some lines and try to keep the forward placement.

---

1 W.E. Brown: Vocal Wisdom, maxims of G. B. Lamperti

BRINGING IT TOGETHER: PLACEMENT, RANGE AND VOLUME

The next exercise will help you to further expand the range and volume of your voice and to prepare it, both in speaking and singing, for a bigger auditorium and/or demanding parts in text or music. Combining placing of the voice and activation of the support, the exercise builds step by step. It's a bit long as well so it might be a good idea to read it through first before you start.

The exercise aims to open up and free the body with help of the inhalations. This freedom and openness is then used to find placement and prolong the phrase length. The exercise is also a good base for high energy voice.

The exercise could easily be known as 'The Exercise that's Very Good for Lots of Things'!

*

We use different parts of the vocal tract to increase our voice's overtones, they help us to project our voice out into the room. While the focus of the earlier exercises has been on the forward area of the vocal tract it's time to open up for the areas a bit deeper in and up in the mouth cavity. We do that by relaxing and opening up the muscles of the neck already during the inhalation.

Step One

In an earlier exercise you inhaled and expanded the area between your pelvis and your back using the image of a rubber band. This time try to envisage the rubber band attached to the pubic bone and the lower part of your skull. The feeling is as if the inhalation continues all the way up to your neck.

Work with the sensation of filling your body with air from the bottom to the top: imagine that the inhaled air drops down to your pelvis, rises to your back and then continues up into the rear of your head.

Let the extension and widening of your back continue up into your neck with the help of the air streaming in. It's imperative that you avoid using tension and muscle activity to force the neck to widen – rather the sensation must be one of the incoming air widening and relaxing the neck from within.

➢ Gently exhale, relax and let the air stream in again.

➢ Keep breathing and prolong each exhalation a little.

   ● Exhale on [f] or [s].
   ● Pay attention to how the release after the exhalation feels in your lower abdomen.

- When the exhalation becomes a bit longer you will notice how your back starts to open during the inhalation.
- A wave of air goes from your lower abdomen through your body and into your back.

➢ Try to see if you can let the inhalation continue all the way up into the back of your head. This wave-like inhalation movement will affect your posture and open up the neck.

➢ When you can clearly feel the widening of back and neck – try to keep the sensation of the widening all through the exhalation. Try with voiced sounds, a lip-trill or even on a vowel.

- Imagine your ribs and back floating or soaring outwards. It is a sensation more than an effort.
- To stay open requires muscle activity, not tension. Release and inhale before any tensions sneak up on you.

➢ Repeat this 'inhale and open' until you have grasped the muscular feeling of it. Allow the inhalation to open your body and keep it open throughout the exhalation. Take as much time as you need and avoid to force the result.

➢ Make a crescendo during the last part of the phrase. Imagine that your rib-cage floats both upwards and sideways. This enables you to keep your body open and ensures that you can access more of the air you have in your lungs.

Remember that you can never empty your lungs completely. But it is easy to tense up and block the air from leaving your body, and thus inhibit your body from using its full capacity.

Be aware of the difference between high-energy physical activity and blocking tensions. Wriggle your shoulders and torso, release tensions in the final part of the exhalation and make sure you don't lock your body.

Step Two

It is crucial to keep the connection between the lower abdomen/pelvis and the open/widened neck throughout the phrase. It is a direction down/out in the pubic area and back/up in the neck area: a feeling of stretching, free from tensions, that goes right through your body between these two points.

During the preparation (i.e. the inhalation) you have adjusted to the most challenging note and level of intensity or the climax of the emotion. The open neck will give you freedom and extra intensity throughout your range.

> Inhale once again and let the air stream down into your pelvis, up to your back and up into your neck.

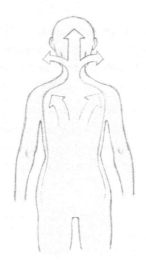

➢ Exhale on a voiced sound [v] or [z] or a lip-trill and keep the back and neck open. The following images might assist you.

- Let the sound come out through the back or top of your head and surf over your crown. Direct the sound to a point in the horizon in front of you.
- It might also help to think that the sound is streaming into your mouth all the way during the sound making. It goes into your mouth, out through the back of your skull and up under the ceiling back to the point far out into the room where it came from.
- Imagine that your upper body is open so that from the pelvis all the way up to the crown is an empty area of air and sound. Keep that huge space open all through the phrase.
- Another image that might help is to consider that the sound streams in through the mouth, into the back of the head, slides around a block and down to the pelvic floor which is where the engine is located.

> ➤ Try the image that helps you the most again, this time while speaking and singing. Keep the feeling that you continuously inhale the phrase. Stay open and free. Slowly expand the phrase in length, range and intensity.

You need to keep an awareness of the muscles all the way from the pelvic floor through your torso and up to the neck. In this way you have contact with the sides when they need to be activated in the sound making. This readiness is a crucial part of the vocal support. Remember the image of the torso having a six-sided breathing box inside.

*

'Breathing' into the neck opens it up, just as the beginning of a yawn does. It opens the rear wall of the pharynx and allows the larynx to drop down – without being pulled down by the extrinsic laryngeal muscles. The dropped down larynx increases the length of the vocal tract and widens the hypopharyngeal space. Your resonance will increase and the harmonies will be more focused, something that brings additional acoustic energy. Your voice will project outwards into the room. The dropped down, lowered larynx also increases the freedom in the vocal folds' movement, which will make it easier for you to hit the high notes and increase the energy in the lowest notes.

The relaxed jaw and tongue slack the upper extrinsic laryngeal muscles and allow the larynx to sink. It is important that you do not lower larynx by pulling it down.

The famous Italian singing teacher Francesco Lamperti pere (1813–92) wrote that all notes, from the highest to the lowest, should be produced by a pillar of air that the singer has perfect control over by holding back the breath. He also wrote that the onset of the sound should be with a light backwards stroke of the glottis, nearly as if one continues the intake of air.[1] The exercises above respond to his ideas

---

1 L'arte del canto (Milan: Ricordi, 1883).

in many ways. 'Holding back the breath' is not really a good way to think: it can create tensions and easily block the free flow of outgoing air. Instead, there should be more of a feeling of focusing the air, intensifying it, and at the same time keeping the airflow going and the subglottal air pressure stable. The 'onset of the sounds with a light backwards stroke' is the same thought as letting the sound stream into the mouth and out through the neck – i.e. the feeling of 'inhaling the sound.'

HIGH ENERGY IN THE VOICE: OUTER AND INNER ENERGY

Here follows an exercise that might seem impossible at first but it is not as difficult as you may think. It will create a higher flexibility in your body and breathing. In both versions of the exercise you move while continuing the airflow and the sound. This should be one gentle, soft, flexible movement: a kind of melting down and thereafter rising up just as softly.

The exercise comes in different variations that build upon each other.

> Start this exercise on a voiced lip-trill. Keep trilling on one exhalation and move from standing ~ sitting ~ lying down ~ moving on the floor ~ sitting ~ standing up ~ sitting ~~. Keep a steady lip-trill throughout the movements. Breathe only when you really need oxygen, rather than when you think you need it.

> Keep trilling while melting down ~ moving on the floor ~ rising up ~~ and pay attention to:

- What kind of movements released your breathing?
- Where in your body did you block your breathing?
- What benefited your voice?
- Find the strategies you need to solve any challenges.

When you feel open, energized, flexible and free from tensions, then it's time to do the same exercise while trilling on a tune. Keep the voice supported and connected.

- ➤ In the first variation of this exercise you breathe where the words and music indicate it, following the phrasing of the text or the song. Can you move between standing ~ lying ~ moving on the floor ~ standing ~~ in singing or speaking without disturbing the airflow or pitch? Pause the movement while breathing.

- ➤ In the second variation you should follow your body's need for air and skip the phrasing of the music or text. Keep trilling the tune regardless of what the text or the music says until your body *really* needs air. Then stop the movement and take the time needed to breathe. Don't be tempted to snatch a little air somewhere in the middle. When you need to breathe, do it properly.

- ➤ Repeat the first variation and notice if the second variation altered anything in your voice or breathing.

- ➤ Now try both variations again, but this time sing with the words. Don't lose the energy in your voice that you gained with the lip-trill.

  - The first time breathe when the song or text has its pauses.
  - Second time only follow your need for air.
  - Then go back to follow the structure and see if anything changed.

- ➤ Continue the exercise and this time say a text out loud. Keep the energy.

*

Bring the flexibility from the exercise above into the next exercise. It is important that you bring with you the placing of the voice and the feeling of lightness. Remember were you finished the Beetle, that is where this exercise starts: standing on the floor moving all your limbs.

➤ Plant your feet firmly on the floor with the body and breathing in full flow. 'Glue' your feet to the floor and try to challenge yourself in how balanced you are. How much can you bend, tilt and turn without losing your steadiness or the stability of the airflow? Imagine seaweed, with the roots deep into the seabed and the branches moving with the water. You can go from a gentle swell to full storm.

➤ Remember that the movement needs to have a focus, to go in one direction at a time, even if it subsequently changes quickly.

➤ Play with your voice in conjunction with the movements. Start on a voiced lip-trill. Let the energy and the direction of your body coordinate with the sound. They shall have the same direction. There is a start, a journey and a finishing goal for your movement and sound.

➤ When the trilling feels comfortable, take an [m] and open for a vowel 'mmmOoo.' Change vowel whenever you like. It is important to work on as many sounds as possible.

➤ Challenge yourself with the duration of the sounds and movements. As always, stop before you tense up.

➤ Play with different qualities of the movements and sounds in the exercises above:

- lyrical and soft with legato;
- dramatic and sharp with staccato;
- mix them by changing quality often and on one exhalation.

➢ Try the different qualities in singing and speaking.

How have your breathing, voice, range and duration been affected by the different versions?

➢ In the next step stop the movement in your body some-where in the middle of the activity, but keep the energy and direction in your voice. This is trickier than it seems. Pay attention – neither block nor force the airflow or the voice. Let the energy start from the floor, travel within your body and flow out through your mouth.

This exercise allows you to practice the skill of keeping a high energy within the body, even when your 'outer' body is still. This high inner energy is necessary when you have to produce high energy voice with a 'non-moving' body. When the 'outer' body is still we easily become passive 'inside' the body too. Hence there is no motor for the voice and we tend to force it instead. Going from high energy outside and inside to low energy outside, with maintained high energy inside, is important to master. Part of being able to do this is to keep the clear direction of the voice – the need to be listened to, the eagerness to be understood – even when the 'outer' body is at peace.

HIGH ENERGY IN THE VOICE AND BODY: BUILDING STRENGTH

We continue with an exercise for high energy voice production which will benefit those who need to use their voice during physical work such as dancing. The exercise helps you to keep a stable airflow and voice during more intense movements. If you are out of breath due to low endurance or fitness, no breathing technique will help you to compensate for that – alas, you just have to start exercising!

In this exercise you will work with high energy but stay free from blocking tensions. The exercise might seem harder than it actually is. However, it does take a certain amount of energy and determination so take a rest whenever you feel you need one.

As in most exercises don't interfere with the inhalation. Trust your body.

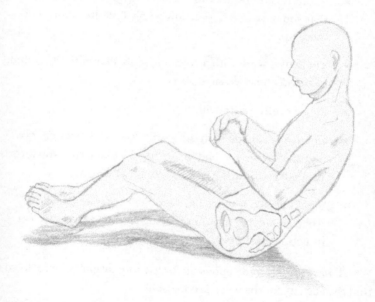

➢ Sit on your buttocks with your bent legs lifted. Find a position where you sit a bit behind your sit bones but still in front of your tailbone.

● Balance your body into a reasonably comfortable position. We are not doing sit-ups – if it feels too heavy, keep your knees a little closer to your chest.

- Bend your neck slightly forwards to release your neck and throat from tensions.
- During the sound making softly wriggle your pelvis and hips to remain free from tensions.

Keep the forward placement and lightness of the voice. It will help you to free the sound and release your vocal folds.

➢ In this position start with a voiceless lip-trill. Make sure that you have a steady airflow going. Breathe before you tense up.

➢ Thereafter work with a voiced lip-trill. Play with the sound: *glissandi* and a *Messa di Voce*.

➢ Sing a tune on a lip-trill.

➢ Change to singing with the words. Keep the same energy and air-flow as you had in the lip-trill. Make sure you direct your voice towards a specific point in the room.

➢ Finally speak. You need to keep the energy and air-flow from the singing in your speaking as well. Having a clear direction for the voice helps you with this.

Which part of your body opens up for the inhalation? Where do you find the activity for the voice production?

In this exercise your abdominal muscles are active and enable you to keep your position. Notice how the muscles of the back step in for the breathing. These back muscles are important for a high energized voice production. Try to keep the awareness and activity from the exercise once you're up on your feet again.

SHOUTING AND SCREAMING

When it comes to shouting or screaming, and to be able to do that in a vocally safe way, we need to prepare both the body and mind carefully. In real life we only shout or scream when it is absolutely necessary. We shout to warn or to attract attention. In such situations the *need* to shout, the impulse to do it, prepares the body. The expansion of the body and the inhalation respond to that impulse. As long as we don't inhibit that impulse the voice will come out free and ringing. If you see a child running out into the street, just as a car approaches, you will shout a warning. There is no hesitation, no 'what will people think' – just the impulse to warn taking over and allowing you to shout. The sound is free and loud because you don't have any blocking thoughts in your mind.

It's the same with screaming. We scream because of fear or pain, physical or emotional. The scream is a release of emotions. The need for that release allows us to scream in a fully bodily engaged way, as long as our 'social selves' do not interfere and block the sound. We seldom scream in real life. On the rare occasions when we do scream, such as a major crisis, we have no alternative other than to scream – otherwise we feel we will die or go mad. That form of screaming is also done with a fully engaged body and mind.

On stage, we must find this need for the shouting or the screaming, and be brave enough to embrace the situation and to let the sound out. Techniques for shouting and screaming start with finding the reason to do it. Where does that reason/impulse come from? What is the situation? If you can't find a really good reason to scream or shout, I would like to suggest that you find another form of expression. Personally, I find that too many of the screams on stage are unnecessary.

The exercises of the 'va' (p. 105) together with the previous exercise about placing of the voice is the base for shouting. As always, the sound surfs on top of the air pillar; imagine that it comes with such a force, a need to come out, that it erupts like a volcano from your guts, hits the ceiling of your mouth and bounces out. The same goes for screaming. A true scream is in my experience a clearer and more free sound than we usually imagine. The vocal scratching sound we hear in movies and on stage is an imitation of a scream. The really genuine screams are free sounds, sounds from when the body takes over from the mind and lets out a sound that's required for survival. Technically they are similar to high energy calling or shouting, with the whole body involved and engaged in the sound making.

The louder you are, the more energy your voice has, the more urgency and energy your words and articulation must have as well. The energy of the words and articulation must be in balance with the energy of your voice.

Warming Up the Voice

THE DAILY ROUTINE

It is very important that you take care of your instrument with a warming up before rehearsals and performances. I like to stress before the rehearsals – it's often the case that you work longer days and harder in rehearsals than in an actual performance. A daily warming up, also in periods of less work, is a good routine to have. With that daily training you keep your body and voice in a basic fitness. This will make it much easier to quickly raise the level of your vocal fitness into a professional state when you need it. Make warming up a routine but not in routine.

If you are preparing for a performance you will also need to adjust the warming up to the task ahead. Vocally demanding part or not? Speaking, singing or both? The range of the part? Challenging movements such as dancing or fencing? The auditorium: big, small or tricky acoustics?

Warming up the voice is to warm up the vocal apparatus, not the vocal folds. You can do whatever exercises you like as long as you remember that the airstream is the fuel for the voice. A free body benefits the breathing → the breathing is the source for the sound → the sound is amplified by the resonators and moulded into speech sounds by the articulators.

Remember that warming up the voice is to prepare for and get ready for work: it is warming up, not working out. If you are in good shape vocally it will not take more than fifteen to twenty minutes.

A warm up will help you to tackle what is ahead of you effortlessly and with confidence.

Just as you warm up before you work don't forget to 'warm down' your body and mind afterwards. Hum, or lip-trill, gently through your range for several minutes. Finish somewhere in your speaking voice, still with a high placing of the resonance.

Go back through the book and pick the exercises that you have enjoyed and that have worked for you. Simplify them if you want to but don't get careless. Keep in mind that when your body and breathing are warmed up, then your voice is warmed up as well. Build your warm-up step by step and don't be tempted to rush.

- Start with the foundation of your balance that gives you freedom for your body and breathing.
- Work towards the fully projected voice.
- Add some energized articulation.

Work with focus and give those parts of your body that need it a bit more attention.

Here comes a suggestion for a warming up.

➢ How are you standing (or sitting or lying)?

- Firmly planted feet?
- Unlocked ankles, knees, hips?
- Balanced spine?
- Free and hanging shoulders?
- Free and hanging jaw?
- Relaxed tongue, resting on the floor of the mouth?
- Floating head?

If anything is tensed or not free take your time to release before you continue.

➢ How is your breathing?

- Where is the breathing in your body? In your abdomen, lower back, sides, chest, higher back?
- Have you noticed any tensions or blockings?
- Are you breathing quickly or slowly?

Make sure that your breathing has access to your entire torso. Slowly expand your exhalation and pay attention so that you keep your body free and flexible even when the exhalation grows longer. Take the time needed to let the body open up for each new inhalation: abdomen – pelvic area – back – neck.

➢ Energize the breathing with a voiceless lip-trill. Expand your breath and keep the trill going. Let the body move softly to avoid any blockage. Expanding your exhalation will help you to open up for the free and active inhalation.

➢ Add voice and trill trough your comfortable range.

➢ Keep working and add a *Messa di Voce*, throughout your range.

Here is another version of warming up when your body is ready and it is time for the voice.

➢ Start making a soft sound. Inhale on a soft yawn and exhale on a soft sigh: 'hoy≈oy≈oy.' Gently sneak the vocal folds into action with help of the airstream.

- Let the yawn grow a little bit bigger each time. Make sure that it finally opens your neck as well. Keep the expanded and relaxed neck in the 'hoy≈oy≈oy.'

- Pay attention to the flexibility and freedom of the rear part of your tongue in the [y] sound, as well as the jaw: 'chew' a bit on the sound. The [y] sound will make the rear part of the tongue lift a bit from the pharynx.
- Expand the length of the phrase; add more 'oy.' Change the vowel before the [y] now and then 'oy, ay, uy, ey...'
- Gently build your vocal energy and direct the sound further and further away from you. Make sure your breathing is connected to the sound making all the time. The inhalation prepares for the sound to come, and the exhalation carries the sound on top of the air.
- Work through your range, both in your modal voice and in your falsetto. Keep the focused laser beam voice in mind. The sound is centred, slim and light. It does not spread.
- Add some active articulation to warm up your articulators. Keep the voice supported with the air stream.

If it is a sluggish day and your body is reluctant to get into gear or get into working mood then you could begin with a Beetle and combine it with the lip-trill. Start on the floor and work until you are fully up and energized in body, breathing and voice.

Vocal Health

- Drink water (one to two litres a day). The vocal folds and all the body need to be moisturized. The drier the air, the more water is needed.

- Stop smoking! Smoke dries out and irritates the mucous membranes. Smoking is one of the most damaging things you can do to your vocal folds. When you quit smoking, you will most likely experience problems with coughing and mucus for a long time but this is part of the healing process. Eventually, your voice will get better as will your general fitness.

- Avoid whispering or 'reserving' your voice as a means to conserve it. There is a danger that you will tense up instead. Allow the airflow to be the voice's fuel.

- A throat clearing habit wears out the vocal folds so try to relax the throat instead. Take a sip of water or sigh or make a gentle hum.

- Reflux (regurgitation of acid juice from the stomach) affects the vocal folds. If you have it regularly, see a doctor.

- If you experience an increase in mucus production in your throat this can indicate that you have overworked your voice.

- Don't ignore warning signs such as:
  - ... persistent pain in the throat, especially if you do not have a cold or an infection
  - ... pain when you speak or swallow
  - ... your voice is more tired than usual
  - ... the voice is hoarse and scratchy but you do not have an infection
  - ... your voice showing no signs of recovery after a night's sleep
  - ... if it takes longer than usual to warm up your voice, or the warming up does not feel comfortable.

- If you have persistent vocal problems, seek the assistance of a speech therapist or phoniatrician.

- Steam can make your voice freer and clearer: a hot shower or a warm bath is good for the vocal folds. Alternatively lean over a bowl of hot water – with a towel covering both your head and the bowl – and breathe in the steam for a few minutes.

- Warm up your voice before rehearsal and performance. A few minutes can make a big difference. Also remember to calm down and relax after rehearsal and performance.

- Think about how you use your voice, and what you expose it to, in everyday life. Our vocal folds are always with us and we need to take care of them.

- A tired voice needs warmth, rest and water. What benefits the body benefits the voice as well. If you need to speak then just say the crucial parts and do so in a fully supported voice.

TROUBLESHOOTING

Sooner or later we will all have some vocal trouble be it minor or major. In such circumstances it is sensible to have a troubleshooting guide to use to establish what went wrong. There is often a straightforward explanation: perhaps you didn't get enough sleep or you didn't drink enough water?

- Did you breathe freely and deep while you were speaking?
- Did your body stay open?
- Were your body and mind prepared and warm?
- Did you embrace the situation and the challenge – or did you block yourself?
- How have you been sleeping?
- Have you been over working recently?
- Are you drinking enough water?
- Do you have the early symptoms of a cold? Are there any other health issues (even something as simple as reflux)?
- What's your home life and social life like? Have you experienced any changes recently?

Establishing what caused the problem enables you to find the solution.

Voice and Text

SOMETHING ABOUT ACTING

There is no value in training your voice to be a flexible instrument unless you're going to use it. The goal of the training is to be able to communicate with others. It does not matter if you are an actor or a teacher; the voice work is basically the same.

This chapter mostly concerns text and shows how there are keys to be found in it. Understanding those keys and using them together with our breathing and voice, helps us to make what we say come alive and connect with the listener.

'Words are the actor's tool – as a brush is the painter's'[1]

*

It's easy to get overwhelmed by the idea of theatre as High Art. At such times it's good to remind ourselves that theatre and acting basically is grown-ups playing, just like we all did as kids. As children we knew that it was not real and that we were playing a game. Still, the game was true to us in the moment and we lived in it *as if* it was reality. Similarly, a play or a movie is also a kind of game. This awareness is a prerequisite for us as an audience to go and see a performance. The story feels true in the moment, but we know it is not real. Protected by this awareness we can receive the, sometimes

---

1 Cicely Berry: *The Actor and the Text*

cruel, narrative, without distancing us from it. None of us intervene when Romeo kills himself in despair over Juliet's death. Confronted with the same situation in real life, we'd tell him that all is well, that Juliet is not dead. But in the theatre we don't, because we know this is not reality.

Actors have trained this 'playing talent' into a craft. They have learned how to be sincere and genuine in an imaginary circumstance. Actors have professional skills, know-how and imagination to portray any kind of character. We all, actors and audience, know that the actor playing Hamlet is not actually Hamlet. Still, in the moment we accept the illusion, that (s)he is the Danish prince.

There are elements in the actor's art that are hard to describe. They concern the actor's inner life: imagination, fantasy, empathy – qualities that bring an understanding of lives and experiences beyond the actor's own life. Other things are highly concrete and tangible, such as having strategies and knowledge to find clues and keys to the characters in the text.

*

The words are a linguistic springboard for the acting. It is the fixed point you must start from when you begin the work of investigating a character. The Swedish playwright and actor Staffan Göthe has a brilliant metaphor: the text should be for the actor what the tight-rope is for the funambulist – the very precondition for the performance and the only thing to stick to.

The characters exist only as lines in a play and it is the actor's work to understand the text and to transform the lines into thoughts and actions. As an actor it is your job to bring the text to the audience in as comprehensive a way as possible. Remember that you have probably spent a lot of time reading your lines and reflecting how to perform them. The audience (*audire* Latin for to hear) has only one chance to hear and grasp the lines, and that is when the actor speaks them.

You need strategies for the text work, how to divide it into manageable steps. It is very much a trying out of ideas, ideas that have their base in the text. The solutions may be different with different productions. There is no absolute right or wrong in this work, however the choices made ought to be based in the text.

Don't get alarmed by these 'rules' – they are there to help you, not limit you, with your acting work. Compare it to sheet music. Inside the strict rules of composition the musician can still find a great freedom. You as an actor can find the same freedom inside the 'rules' of text work.

THOUGHTS AND BREATHING

When we speak in a comfortable situation, we all naturally coordinate our thoughts with our breathing. However, under stress, or when we feel uncomfortable, we easily stop breathing deeply and freely. We might also hold back our breathing for fear of being too loud or too emotional. At other times we do the opposite: we push for voice and emotions. This can occur in our private life as well as professionally in front of an audience. The challenge is to stay open and free in our breathing, come what may.

> ➢ Pay attention to your own thinking–breathing–speaking habits. Does your breathing change depending on the situation? Do you sometimes hold your breath?

> ➢ Notice other people's habits. How do they breathe and speak in different situations?

This knowledge is something you can bring with you, when you are ready to portray different characters.

THOUGHTS AND TEXT

When we speak spontaneously a need, a thought or an idea comes first. In the next moment the thought is dressed in words, we inhale and release it as speech. We naturally adjust our breathing to our thinking. We breathe *between* our thoughts. An interesting observation is that when we lose the thought or try to find the right word, we often hold our breath. As soon as we're back on track, we continue on the same breath. It seems that we mostly stick to 'one thought – one breath' when we speak.

When the speaking comes originally from a script the words are there first. This means that the speaking process is reversed, a circumstance that easily makes the breathing less functional. We start in the middle of the spontaneous speaking process, with the words and not with the need or thought behind them. Furthermore, the words are not our own. When we work with text we need to find the thoughts and ideas behind the words; we collaborate with the authors by giving voice to their thoughts and words. 'Finding the thought' isn't an overly complicated process. Trust the author – the thinking has already been done – there is no need to make up anything by yourself at this early stage. Your task is to discover the character's thoughts, as created by the author.

Below is a simple scheme which illustrates this thought-speech structure. A released need or thought will be expressed as an action. This action can be a pure physical action as well as a spoken one and they frequently come together. Here you see the spontaneous speaking process, that starts with a need or a thought, and the reversed one, that starts with the words and go 'backwards' to find the thought behind the words.

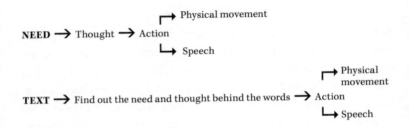

PUNCTUATION WORK

To breathe between the thoughts and only then – just as we do when we speak spontaneously – is a good rule in acting. The starting point in the detective work with the thoughts and text is to identify where one thought ends and another begins. The key to finding this is the punctuation. The end of a thought is marked by a full stop. Other punctuation marks such as semi-colon, exclamation mark or question mark can also indicate this, it depends on the time and context in which the text was written, and on the writer. However, 'one thought – one breath' fits most texts, classic as well as contemporary.

There are also all the other punctuations that give you the opportunity to breathe and phrase the text in an ongoing thought, such as: comma, dash and dot, dot, dot. They each tell you something about how the author imagined the text.

Read the following examples out loud. It is easier to hear and grasp the change in meaning that comes with punctuation when words are spoken, instead of only reading silently and 'hearing' the change in your mind. When you read aloud the changes will be experienced with your body as well as with your intellect. The physical sensation of the words is important in order to bring them to life.

Look at this short dialogue:

> B: 'I want to move to Scotland.'
> C: 'I don't want to leave London.'
> B: 'We can live in Edinburgh. Or Glasgow.'

In this example the full stop after Edinburgh indicates that the thought ends here and then a new thought appears: 'Or Glasgow.'

Compare with this:

> B: 'We can live in Edinburgh or Glasgow.'

Here the line is one thought only. It is more like a suggestion of two possibilities.

When we hold a rest at the commas, without breathing and making a full stop, it shifts the meaning of the text. It will not become a new thought but the tiny 'hold' at the comma emphasizes different aspects of the sentence.

Compare the following sentences and how the content is affected by where the comma is placed:

> A road is a road even in mist.
>
> A road is a road, even in mist.
>
> A road, is a road even in mist.

The pauses and the silence between the words and the phrases give them colour and meaning; do not hesitate to let that space grow.

Now look at these lines:

> If you ever tell anyone about this, I will systematically destroy your
> marriage, reputation, career and life. Something you know I can do.

> If you ever tell anyone about this I will systematically destroy your
> marriage reputation career and life – something you know I can do.

With the first version, take a tiny rest at the commas but only breathe
at the full stop. Let the following sentence become a new thought.
After that, try the second version. Speak the line as one thought only
and on one breath. Do not take a breath at the dash, just hold the
tension for a moment and then continue to the full stop. How do you
perceive/understand the difference between the two versions? Does
the difference in the punctuation change your idea about the motive,
energy or emotions behind the lines? Does the longer line (i.e. where
there is no place to breathe) affect your energy?

BREATHING WITH THE THOUGHTS

When you breathe between the thoughts, and only then, your own
inner tempo and energy will change with the text. If the sentences,
the thoughts, are short and you breathe between every thought, you
will breathe even when you have no real need for air. You will then
notice how your breathing may become more hectic and rushed.
When the length of a sentence is comfortable for you, you will probably get a relaxed breathing. A sentence that is 'too long' will demand
extra energy from your breathing and speaking.

Once you have detected the different thoughts/lines you'll need to
find the reasons behind them – the reasons, not the emotions. Why
does the character say what they are saying? What is the purpose?
What does the character want to achieve with the line? Not only
does this help you find the natural breathing pattern; it will also help

the listener to understand and follow the thoughts or subjects in the text. Here too the answers lie in the text.

While inhaling, you need to prepare for what is ahead of you. Inhale and open up for the need, thoughts, pitch and for the length of the phrase. If you have fully understood your character's need and intention, your body will respond to this and provide the right amount of air. A sentence that is 'too long' will probably not give you any difficulties if you have grasped the full thought and the reason behind it, the energy of it and the character's need to be listened to and understood, before you start to speak. This applies to singing as well: if you have grasped the need and thought behind the words and music, breathing will get easier.

In our everyday life we sometimes skip an inhalation because we are so eager to explain what's on our mind. Usually we finish the sentence anyway, even if it is with a bit of effort. To struggle with a very long line in acting is fine. If we can run out of breath in real life, so can the characters on stage. Most likely the author has a reason behind the length of a thought, a line. A long line often scares us when we read it, however the phrase is seldom as impossible as we feared when we actually say it out loud.

When you memorize text, do so thought by thought. In this way, the text comes into your body in a more organic way and it becomes easier to breathe and act it out organically. Breathing with the text, by following the punctuation, will make you breathe as if you were the character you portray. In this way punctuation helps you with your acting.

*

Our thoughts and our emotions affect our breathing. In acting we can also look at it another way; when we adjust or change our breathing according to the punctuation, we help ourselves connect with and understand the character's energy, needs and state of mind.

We can go one step further and also let the audience understand the situation the character is in, and the character's needs and emotions, through the actor's way of breathing. It is not only *where* we breathe in the text but also *how* we do it which tells the audience something about the character. Your breathing can be deep or shallow, long or short, rhythmic or irregular, calm or hectic, strained or relaxed. This is up to your imagination, as long as you take care of your vocal health. Your breathing is most definitely a part of your acting.

THE SHAPE OF A THOUGHT

We use the words to express a need or a wish. We speak to affect others, to clarify our own thoughts or to release or handle our emotions with the help of the words. We can for example start an argument, develop it and come to a conclusion. This can be done both on our own and in conversation with others. We use the speech as an action; the words affect and change the speaker, the listener and the situation.

Sometimes what we say is not so important, it is just small talk, and the words flow effortlessly. Other times we really choose the words very carefully. Sometimes we are sure about what we think and just say it out loud. Other times we use the words to establish what we actually do think about a subject.

As an actor you need to work out how the character's thoughts take shape. Is the thought clear and already dressed in words and therefore just erupts? Or is the thought formed and shaped while the character is speaking? Is the character very particular with the words or not? This might change between each thought. The answer to such questions lies in the lines and in how the actor understands them. Your answer will affect where you breathe as well as the tempo of your speech.

DIFFERENT DIRECTIONS FOR THE THOUGHT

Thoughts can develop in different directions. As an actor it is important to be aware of how the character's thoughts go. Therein lies the key to the character and the dramatic situation.

- The thoughts follow each other in a consecutive chain. One line follows into the next, as a development of one topic.
- The thoughts change direction completely. They jump from one topic into something totally different and then stay on the new topic.
- The thoughts make a roundabout way into another topic and then come back into the main thought. As an actor it is important to keep the awareness of the main topic in mind, while your character is taking a detour.

Keep an eye out for the words that change the direction of the thought: words such as 'but', 'and', 'however', 'yet,' 'or,' 'although.' These are words that pause the thought, change the direction of it, develop it further, clarify it or add something new to it.

Working with text thought by thought is also, in my opinion, the key to good acting. The words carry the thoughts. It is the idea behind the words that will reach the listener, not just the words themselves. For the words to come alive, you must be aware of the impulse, the need, that triggered the character to speak. Each new need or thought gives a new impulse to speak.

FOCUS WORD

Different ways of emphasizing a thought in a sentence, a line, give different meanings to it. The word you emphasize in each thought is called a focus word.

Here is an example:

I might come here TOMORROW.

I MIGHT come here tomorrow.

In the first version, it is about *when* I might come, in the second it is about *if* I will come at all. Both versions may be right depending on the situation in the play and the actor's choice.

It is easy to put stress on dramatic words. Take the phrase 'You and your bloody jealousy.' Here it is tempting to put the stress on 'bloody' but the line is about 'jealousy.' Try both versions out loud. See which version clarifies the thought best.

You and your BLOODY jealousy.

You and your bloody JEALOUSY.

If it is the first time the jealousy is mentioned that word clarifies the situation and needs to have focus. However, if the character has been talking about jealousy many times already, then 'bloody' might be a good choice.

As a rule, keep to one focus word for each thought. In this way, you are forced to make a clear choice about what the character you portray means/wants/intends.

*

The exercise in capacity where you expand the phrase by adding one more word after each inhalation, is also a good way to find the focus word or a word that affects the thought:

To [inhale]

To be [inhale]

To be or [inhale]...

The exercise makes you 'taste' every word and it helps you discover the value of each word as well as expand your breathing. You will notice when you come to a word that clarifies or changes the meaning of the phrase.

THE WORDS AS KEYS

The choice of words and the way they are expressed reveal something about the character. They are keys for the actor to think about. What words has the author chosen and why exactly these words and no other words? They can tell you a lot about the character: social position, background, self-esteem, education, politeness, intelligence. Singing is also speaking – but you deliver the words on pitch and in rhythm. You can ask the same questions for both the words and the music. What notes has the composer chosen: high notes, low notes, forte or pianissimo? Why is that specific word on a high note, a long note or stretched out over many notes? The questions are limitless.

However, every word is not equally important and as a performer you need to make choices. Trying to make every word equally important and alive makes acting impossibly difficult and something rather different from the fluency of real life.

It is not only your own character's words that are important. The words of the other characters provide you with information as well. It is very important to actively listen to them. You need to sincerely listen, not act 'I am listening now.' You need to listen with fresh ears during every performance. If you listen to the other actors' words, they will affect you and help you with your own acting. It is in the other characters' words you find the fuel for your own forthcoming response.

As an actor, when you portray a character, what do you think when you hear what the others say? What word is it that you react to or respond to? What word changes the direction of your thoughts? Where, on what word in the other actors' lines, does your impulse to inhale for your response start?

To make this organic, you need to be very clear about the goals, needs and plans of your character. What is the situation? What are the character's goals, both in the present moment and in the long term? Goals might change during the play. Bear in mind that you, as actor, know things that the character does not know. You need to be in the moment and act the situation, not the story.

*

I find that trusting the words, and the author, is something that is in decline nowadays, as if the thoughts and words are not interesting enough as they are. Give the words a chance – taste them, experience them, mean them and allow them to affect you while you say them. If you fully understand the text and stay connected to the words while speaking, they will affect both you, your co-actors and the audience. They will do an important part of your acting job for you. You can in a way surf on top of the words, carried onward in the acting by them.

ARTICULATION

The more eager we are to be heard and understood, the clearer we articulate. That is something we all do naturally. This seems to be applicable in all cultures and languages; high energy articulation signals that something important is being said. We put our need to be understood into the energy of our articulation.

Precise articulation can be used to tell the audience that what is being said is important (to the character). I must say that I've hardly ever heard anyone mumble in real life as much as some actors do on stage and screen in their aim to sound 'natural.' Sloppy articulation, in my opinion, only sends the signal that what is being said is not important.

My old acting teacher once said to me, half joking, half serious: 'If you have been struggling for a long time with a line and still feel that you haven't fully grasped it; articulate with confidence and have a clear direction when you speak. The audience will then think that you know what you are saying and they will most likely understand the line – even if you don't.' I'd like to add that sometimes trusting in the beauty or music in the language might be enough. Don't be afraid of giving in to, and enjoying, bygone days' way of expressing thoughts with poetry or beauty, texts from a time when thoughts were expressed more elaborately than we take the time to do today.

Articulation is also an excellent tool when portraying different characters. Changing your way of speaking, such as tempo, fluency and articulation, is better than changing your voice to fit the character you portray. Keeping your own voice will give you a bigger freedom in expressions and nuances and benefit your vocal health. Also, there is nothing like an 'old man's' or 'an innocent girl's' voice. Ideas like that can easily result in stereotypes. On the other hand, remember that it is the actor who needs to have a good vocal technique, not the character. There is no need to sound as if the character has a great voice, as long as you use your voice in a healthy way.

Another aspect is that your articulation and voice must match the situation the character is in. This is especially important to remember when you have a microphone, such as in acting for the camera. The energy of your voice and articulation must fit the character's intention. For instance, if your character is talking to a large group of people, you as an actor cannot have an intimate 'microphone' voice or a soft articulation. You need to use the same amount of energy as the character would have needed without such equipment.

How you articulate will not only tell the audience something about the character; it will also stimulate and help you as an actor to come into contact with the words, the needs and intentions of your character.

There is a neurological two-way information between the brain and the muscles. A thought or emotion initiates neurological impulses that go from the emotional centre and the 'language department' in the brain via the motor-cortex to the articulation muscles. It happens the other way around as well. When you articulate with energy and precision the motor-cortex sends impulses to the other parts of the brain with the information that what you are saying is important. In other words, you yourself get affected by your own articulation.

ACTING

'A dramatic situation, a scene, consists of a series of actions. These are necessary for the actor. 'I have to know what I do.' The actor's tool is not primarily her feelings, but her actions. Feelings are there of course but are fickle and need physical actions to be readable for the audience. Through my way of performing an action, an audience can understand if I'm in love or broken with sadness. Actions are concrete. For the action to become alive, one must become aware of the impulse, the need, that triggered it. The actor's art is not improvisation but the art of repeating, evening after evening, without ending in dead routine and mechanical actions. To stay open to, in relation to, and conscious of the needs and impulses that drive the character forward is the first step towards achieving this.'

Birgitta Vallgårda, Professor emerita
Malmö Theatre Academy, Lunds Universitet

We can put it this way: *what* action I perform, *how* I do it and *when* I do it depends on *why* I do it. I think this probably applies to everyday life as well as acting.

On stage or before the camera we are still ourselves. We portray the characters; we lend our bodies and voices to them. We should think the thoughts that stimulate us to react *as if* we were in the character's situation. This way of working with our thinking on stage is reliable. Then we are not dependent on our feelings in the work. Feelings come and go and are not trustworthy or repeatable. However, if we can master our thinking we have a stable tool for our acting. Our thinking will then be as reliable as our physical actions on stage.

The challenge is to find the balance between involvement and control. Struggling too much with thinking the character's thoughts or with feeling the character's feelings will easily make you self-absorbed with your inner life instead of listening and connecting with your fellow actors. It disconnects you from the situation in the scene. An audience that doesn't understand the situation can easily find an over-emotional actor more embarrassing than touching, or simply lose interest in what is happening on stage. Emotions will come and go; they are all part of the work. Don't strive for them to come and do not evaluate them. Just let the emotions be there.

A good argument against the idea that an actor must feel the character's feelings are cartoons. The cartoon characters have no feelings of their own nevertheless they do affect us through their physical actions, their behaviour, and our understanding of the situation they are in.

It is not the actor who will have an experience – it is the audience. How you make that happen does not really matter. What is important is to let the audience understand the situation and the relations between the characters on stage. Through that understanding the audience's own imagination will start to work, and their thoughts and emotions will be stimulated. In this way the actor and the audience will cooperate and an exchange of energy between stage and auditorium will arise. That is why each performance is unlike any other. This interaction between actors and audience is vital. One can even say that there are just as many different versions of the play as there are people in the audience. We all see and understand the performance based on our own experiences and understanding of life.

*

Characters do not exist outside the play. They are the creation of an authors' mind expressed as words on a piece of paper, and have no past and no future. It is important that we don't put our own values on the character. I sometimes encounter the idea that 'my character would never do that.' I think this comes from when the actor does not differentiate clearly enough between themselves and the character. In order to gain a greater freedom in your artistic choices you have to leave the limiting thoughts of what the character can or cannot do. What might seem highly illogical from the outside, from the actor's personal perspective, can be very logical from the character's point of view.

Finally, I would like to encourage you to keep an open mind in your work. Don't decide too much about your character until far into the rehearsals. Work with the attitude that it is not until the last performance that you have finally fully understood your character. This will provide the motivation for you to keep on investigating and making new discoveries about your character through all the performances.

Epilogue

By now I hope that you have gained a good understanding of how the voice functions. From science to practical exercises you will have built an awareness of your own voice. In the end, you will be the one who knows your voice best, what you can or cannot do with it and how much rest and care your voice needs.

My old acting teacher always said that there is no 'Method' about how to act. Every actor needs to find their own way, their own method. I will say that the same goes for voice work. You need to be methodological when you learn about your voice and how it functions, but there is no one-and-for-all method or exercise in the discovery of your voice.

The section about vocal science is included to give you a basic understanding about the function of the body. Hopefully, this knowledge will give you a deeper understanding of the exercises so you can perform them as effectively as possible.

It's not talent alone that makes a great artist, rather it's the earnest disciplined work that allows talent to develop into a profession. Being an artist is an ongoing occupation: you can never cease to learn, nurture and maintain skills and knowledge. This is not exactly new understanding: Geoffrey Chaucer (1343–1400) said 'Thy lyf so short, the craft so long to lerne.'

Mind and body must work together, so you need to stay present in the exercises even when they bore you. There is no intrinsic value in exercises, if any of them don't work for you simply skip or adjust them. The point is not to be good at doing exercises, but rather understand what they achieve; freedom in your communication and in your voice, both in your personal and professional life.

Bibliography

Alipour, F., Jaiswal, S. & Finnegan, E., *Acoustic and aerodynamic effects of false folds and epiglottis*, (The Journal of the Acoustical Society of America, vol. 120: 3354. 2006).

Aronson, A. E., *Clinical Voice Disorders*, (3rd ed.), (New York: Thieme, 1990).

Bailly, L., Bernardone, N., Müller F., Rohlfs, K. & Hess, M., *Ventricular-Folds Dynamics in Human Phonation*, (Journal of Speech, Language and Hearing Research, vol. 57: 1219–42. 2014).

Beckman, M., *Shakespeare, Molière och andra*, (Lund: Liber, 1984).

Berry, C., *The Actor and the Text*, (London: Virgin Books, 1992).

Biggs, J., *Teaching for Quality Learning at University*, (2nd ed.), (UK: Open University Press, 2003).

Bjerstedt, S. & Emgård, H., *Reflektioner om reflektion: Något om skådespelarutbildningens reflektionsuppgifter*, (Lunds Universitet, 2013).

Brown, W. E., *Vocal Wisdom, maxims of G. B. Lamperti*, (New York: Taplinger Publishing Company, 1957).

Delvaux, B. & Howard, D. M., *On the epilarynx dimensions for voice classification*, (University of York, 2015).

Denes, P. B. & Pinson, E. N., *The Speech Chain*, (Bell Telephone Laboratories Inc. New York, 1963).

Dropsy, J., *Den harmoniska kroppen* (*Le corps bien accordé*), (Viborg: Natur & Kultur, 1997).

Emgård, H., *Countertenor jämförd med falsett*, (Lunds Universitet, 1997).

Eriksson, N. & Rödseth Smith, S., *Påverkas röstkällans egenskaper av förändrad stående kroppshållning? En experimentell studie av otränade mansröster*, (Göteborgs Universitet, 2013).

Furn, A-C., *Professionell röstanvändning i läraryrket*, (Lund: Studentlitteratur, 2017).

Garcia, M., (compilation, revision and translation D. V. Paschke), *A Complete Treatise on the Art of Singing*, (*Traité complet de l'art du chant*: 1841, 1872), (New York: Da Capo Press, 1984).

Gibbs, G., *Learning by Doing: a guide to teaching and learning methods*, (Oxford: Further Education Unit, 1988).

Göthe, S., *Lysande eländen*, (Paris: Schultz Förlag AB, 2003).

Greene, M. & Mathieson, L., *The Voice and its Disorders*, (6th ed.), (London: Whurr Publishers, 2001).

Iwarsson, J., *Breathing and Phonation – Effects of Lung Volume and Breathing Behaviour on Voice Function*, (Stockholm: Department of Clinical Sciences, 2001).

Klingfors, G., *Nytt om gammal sång*, (Stockholm: Gehrmans musikförlag, 1990).

Kolb, D., *Experiential Learning*, (New Jersey: Prentice-Hall, 1984).

Ladefoged, P., *Three areas of experimental phonetics*, (London: Oxford University Press, 1967).

Ladefoged, P. & Maddieson, I., *The Sounds of the World's Languages*, (Oxford: Blackwell Publishing, 1996).

Lieberman, P. & Blumstein, S. E., *Speech physiology, speech perception and acoustic phonetics*, (Cambridge: Cambridge University Press, 1988).

Lindblad, P., *Rösten*, (Lund: Studentlitteratur, 1992).

Rodenburg, P., *The Right to Speak*, (London: Methuen Drama, 1991).

Schneider, B., van Trotsenburg, M., Hanke, G., Bigenzahn, W. & Huber, J., *Voice impairment and menopause*, (Menopause, 11[2]: 151–8. 2004).

Shewell, C., *Voice work: art and science in changing voices*, (Chichester: Wiley-Blackwell, 2009).

Simberg, S., *Resonansrörsmetoden – en kort överblick av användningen av resonansrör i vatten*, (Puhe ja kieli, 35[3]: 127–136. 2015).

Sonninen, A., *The external frame function in the control of pitch in the human voice*, (Annuals of the New York Academy of Sciences, vol.155 [1], 68–90. 1968).

Stanislavskij, K., *Arbetet med rollen (Rabota aktera nad rol' jo)*, (Tallin: Sahlgren Förlag AB, 1997).

Stark, J. A., *Bel Canto: a History of Vocal Pedagogy*, (Toronto: University of Toronto Press, 2003).

Stewart, C. F., Kling, I. F. & Allen, E. L., *Voice Rehabilitation*, (Burlington: Jones & Bartlett Learning, 2016).

Sonesson, B., *Anatomi*, (Stockholm: AWE/Gebers, 1974).

Sonesson, B., *Tillämpad anatomi*, (Stockholm: Liber, 1975).

Sundberg, J., *Röstlära – fakta om rösten i tal och sång*, (Stockholm: Proprius, 1986).

Sundberg, J. & Skoog, J., *Dependency of jaw opening on pitch and vowel in singing*, (Journal of Voice 11[3]: 301–6. 1997).

Titze, I. R., *Principles of voice production*, (Denver: National Centre for Voice and Speech, 1994).

Unné Göransson, M. & Emgård, H., *Grundläggande röstarbete*, (Lunds Universitet, 2008).

Vennard, W., *Singing, the Mechanism and the Technic*, (New York: Carl Fischer, 1967).